12^{45}

To Dad
with love,

Lance

(Christmas of '81)

in respectful memory of S. Arieti

Abraham and the Contemporary Mind

Other books by Silvano Arieti *

THE INTRAPSYCHIC SELF

(1967)

THE WILL TO BE HUMAN

(1972)

CREATIVITY: THE MAGIC SYNTHESIS

(1976)

LOVE CAN BE FOUND (*with James Arieti*)

(1977)

THE PARNAS

(1979)

* Books of exclusive psychiatric interest are not included.

ABRAHAM
AND THE
CONTEMPORARY
MIND

Silvano Arieti

Basic Books, Inc., Publishers

NEW YORK

The author gratefully acknowledges permission to use the following material:

A quotation from Dante Alighieri, *The Divine Comedy,* translated, with a commentary by Charles Singleton. Bollingen Series LXXX. Volume 3: *Paradiso* copyright © 1975 by Princeton University Press. Reprinted by permission of Princeton University Press.

The following photographs that appear facing each chapter opening: A portion of Ghiberti's *Sacrifice of Isaac* from the Baptistry in Florence (chapter 1); a portion of Donatello's *Abraham and Isaac* (chapter 3); and a fresco of the *Sacrifice of Iphigenia* from Pompey (chapter 5)—all by permission of Alinari Fratelli SpA Istituto di Edizioni Artistiche, via Nazionale 6, Florence, Italy.

Plate 20 of the *Sacrifice of the Patriarch Abraham* from *Tiziano e la silografia veneziana del cinquecento,* copyright © by Neri Pozza Editore, Vincenza 1976 (chapter 2).

William Tell, anonymous nineteenth-century wood engraving, probably British, from the Print Collection, The New York Public Library, Astor, Lenox, and Tilden Foundations (chapter 4).

Library of Congress Cataloging in Publication Data

Arieti, Silvano.
    Abraham and the contemporary mind.

    Includes bibliographical references and index.
    1. Abraham, the patriarch. 2. Psychology—
Philosophy. 3. Civilization, Modern—20th
century. I. Title.
BS580.A3A74   222'.11'0924   80-68187
ISBN: 0-465-00005-3

To my two-year-old granddaughter
Aviva,
with the faith that one day
she will discover
these pages.

CONTENTS

PREFACE

Must a man who is neither a professional Bible scholar nor a theologian nor a philosopher apologize for discussing the story of Abraham and for trying to show the relevance of the story to the basic issues of our time? I believe not. What has inspired me to do so has occupied an important place in my heart and my mind for a long time. And because I have long and intimately related the great historical heritage with the experiences of my own life and with the fields in which I have acquired some particular competence, I feel entitled to set out on this journey.

Although by training a physician, a psychiatrist, and a psychoanalyst, I have always tried to understand the connection between my professional work and the various philosophical, aesthetic, social, and political issues of our day. In particular, I have been interested in the problem of creativity. This time I am attempting something new. We live in an unstable, disturbing, and dangerous cultural climate in which people seem to have lost some of their bearings and values or to have abandoned themselves to total disenchantment with the past or to despair or at least to being skeptical about the future. In such a climate any effort to relocate our sense of purpose, any attempt to inspire and to reacquire faith might, it seems to me, be welcome. It is in this spirit that I offer the present book to my contemporaries and to the generations that follow.

I have here tried to present the story of Abraham for modern man. I am not so presumptuous as to believe that I have solved all the issues raised in this book, but neither am I so humble as to deny my own sense of surprise experienced in the writing of it or the sensation of having been inspired or the desire to transmit to others at least some part of these feelings.

SILVANO ARIETI
July 1980

CHAPTER

I

Revelation, Dualism, Sanctification

Detail of the Sacrifice of Isaac by Ghiberti

At dusk when the earth seems to quiver, the swallows joyfully circle the air, and in the velvet sky there is an expectation of the first stars. The trees, the bushes, and the grass, thirsty for dew, welcome the arriving night with their fragrances. Once at such an hour, three to four thousand years ago, between spring and summer, in an obscure part of the Near Orient, a forty-eight-year-old man from the land of Ur feels as if he is being penetrated by the glory of all that he can see, hear, smell, and touch, and by the rest of the universe that he can think of and imagine.

Like his contemporaries, this man from Ur feels possessed by that which surrounds him, as if not only the birds and the bushes, but the setting sun and the rising stars and the waves of the sea breaking on the rocky shores and the brook of the valley and the soft wind are all animated by some kind of inner life.

But then suddenly and yet calmly, in recognition of something that has been growing inside him for a long time, he feels he must for a few moments at least silence all earthly sounds, close his eyes to the glory of all celestial and terrestrial colors and close his mind to the unseen spaces and the unlived times. And as he does so, his ephemeral grasp touches the eternal: with his inner ear he can hear the eternal voice, the invisible appears to him in an invisible way, and the unthinkable becomes part of his thoughts. Even all the echoes of the human songs of sorrow and joy fade away and are replaced by a hymn, audible only to him, which sings of a greater harmony, a greater beauty, a greater justice, and of love.

This is the revelation granted to Abram, son of Terah—a revelation in its promised embrace bigger than the cosmos, permitting him as it does the intuition of something greater than the physical universe he knows, an essence separable from the world and yet eternally involved with it in a continuing state of care and love.

Abram's revelation comes to him as the result of something that has been growing inside him for a very long time, from his early childhood. As a young child one night he had looked up at the stars in the sky over the land of Ur, which is midway between the Euphrates and the Persian Gulf, and had had the same feelings as did many other persons in those days. "These are the gods I must adore," he said to himself. But dawn came and the stars faded away. When the sun rose he said, "This is my god." But the sun too disappeared at dusk, and night followed; and then he praised the moon, until it too became invisible. This was the beginning of a search that was to go on and on until the moment of his great revelation.

With his revelation Abram becomes the first Jew—the first man to believe in a single incorporeal God, a God of wonder, beauty, love, and mercy. Although Abram loves nature and responds exuberantly to the richness it offers to his senses and to the processes of his mind, he is able to set aside all these offers to his senses and to the inquiries of his mind and to open himself to the One Great Offer, the One Great Exploration.

But Abram does not only become the first Jew; he also becomes the first modern man. The first *modern* man? Is it possible to accept the notion that a man who lived three to four thousand years ago can be called a "modern" man? This book will try to demonstrate that through that first revelation and because of other deeds, which will be described and discussed later, Abram, despite his antiquity, belongs to the modern world. Many of our own contemporaries are in some respects less modern than Abram, failing as they do to accept or to abide by all that is implied by Abram's intuitions and actions.

First, a few words of clarification. What I have to say about Abraham is not addressed to Jews only, nor is it my aim to proselytize. This is a book written by someone who freely confesses that he does not practice his religion in an orthodox way. My purpose is to reexamine the basic questions raised in every life by the Abraham story. Transient is the passage of man in this world, where he may be an alien, a sojourner, a full participant, or a creative force; but no matter in what historical era his passage takes place, the same questions and the answers to them suggested here find a home for themselves in man's spirit.

If I make the seemingly astonishing statement that Abram in his experience of revelation became a modern man, it is because numberless generations before Abram and numberless generations after him did not conceive the existence of a spiritual entity that could be separated from nature. Idolatry and later, to almost the same extent, paganism, subordinated spirit to nature. Not only in the number of idols and deities worshipped were the beliefs of the ancients distinguished from the intuition of Abram, but also in the fact that for them whatever was divine was immanent, that is, part of nature; for Abram the divine both transcended and preceded nature.

In this chapter I shall discuss the implications of these

two different confrontations with life, the self, the world, the divine. But first we must grapple with a question that my account of Abram may already have roused in the minds of many readers. In describing Abram's moment of revelation, I have spoken of the first of the Hebrew patriarchs as if the biblical account were a historically validated fact. Have I confused documented history with myth?

THE VALUE OF MYTH:
ITS RELATION TO HISTORY AND ART

To begin with, then, it must be said that I accept the notion that the biblical account of Abram-Abraham is a myth.*

Thus I must now stop to discuss certain aspects of the nature of myths in general. What follows is not an exhaustive discussion of the subject but takes into consideration only those aspects of it which are pertinent to the scope of this book.

There have, of course, been many studies aimed at elucidating the origin and the essential characteristics of myths. Most such studies need not concern us here. For example, although the question is extremely pertinent to other types of inquiry, for us it would not be important whether the myth originated full-blown all at once or represented an agglomeration of various fragments taken from different sources, or whether the myth was mainly the creation of a

---

* Since we see in Genesis that Abram was to become Abraham, and to continue to be known as Abraham, from now on I shall simply refer to him as Abraham, even when discussing events that preceded his change of name.

single person or of a group of people or of a special type of society. Similarly, it is not important for us to determine how much of the myth is only the expression of a primordial mentality, say, or of a psychological need or of the return to an infantile conception of the world; nor need we determine whether the myth is only a narrated dream or a projection of the mind or a primitive incestuous fantasy repressed and disguised by a different manifest content. We shall not go into the question of whether the myth is merely an image, a kind of icon, to which has been attributed a given meaning. We shall not even consider the special language in which it has been written down, that is, the etymological origin of the words used or the literary forms of its narration.

For our purposes what matters about the myth is its meaning and its values. We shall be concerned not with the primitive origin of a particular myth but with its greatness. We shall not accept the claim, first expressed in the writings of Aristotle, that no dialogue is possible between reason (or logos) and myth; on the contrary we shall to some extent follow Vico, who saw a special authentic truth in myth, Schelling, who detected in it the possible revelation of the Absolute, and Cassirer, who in his late writings saw myth as a sentimental form imbued with the most powerful human impulses.

To put it another way, we shall be in a position somewhat similar to that of a person reading the *Iliad* for its meaning and value only, leaving to others such tasks as determining whether the epic was written by Homer or by many people over an extended period of time and studying the particular words used, their origin, sequence, repetitions, and the special metrical form. Before returning to the myth of Abraham, therefore, let us begin by examining briefly those technical aspects of myth in general which are pertinent to the subject of this book.

A myth need not be either accepted or rejected because it is a myth. Like everything else, there are good myths, which enhance the human spirit, and (as we shall see particularly in chapter 2) there are bad myths, which themselves provide the ground for tragic realities.

But what *is* a myth? Webster defines it mainly as "A traditional story of unknown authorship, ostensibly with a historical basis, but serving usually to explain some phenomenon of nature, the origin of man, or the customs, institutions, religious rites, etc., of a people; myths usually involve the exploits of gods and heroes." * Let us examine this definition carefully. "A traditional story," it says, "ostensibly with a historical basis." The crux of the matter hinges on the word "ostensibly"; in other words, the possibility of a basis in historical fact is not absolutely or categorically excluded, although the definition implies that most likely the story, *in the form in which it has been transmitted*, does not reflect a historical event.

Among the characteristics of a great myth, or of a myth at least worth considering, are the following. After one removes from it all the trimmings, exaggerations, and traditional elements that have been added over the course of time, at least some parts of what remains seem plausible, or acceptable, literally or metaphorically. Even if the myth cannot simply be accepted as an account of reality, it has content that either could be real under certain circumstances or whose reality cannot be absolutely excluded, or its content is an acceptable imaginative representation of

* *Webster's New World Dictionary of the American Language* (New York and Cleveland: World, 1972).

reality. To give an example, those of us who do not accept the Bible literally find it hard to believe that Abraham lived to the age of one hundred and seventy-five. Perhaps the biblical writer wanted to stress that Abraham lived to be very old and that all the events that gave such astounding uniqueness to his life took place when he was a mature man. We must also stress that even when a myth is based on puny and dubious history, it may become a great myth because it acquires a *historical reality* and value of its own. A myth may generate a series of other myths and in its turn be transformed by them.

The great nineteenth-century Hebrew writer and thinker Ahad Haam wrote that the historical reality of the life of Moses cannot be proved. But even if Moses never existed in fact, he has through the ideas, the feelings, and the actions attributed to him in some sense truly existed in and affected the life of the Jewish people for thousands of years. The same thing could of course be said for Abraham—as well as for Buddha, Jesus, and other religious innovators. The historical reality of Jesus also stands on shaky ground, though not quite as shaky as that of Abraham and Moses. (The only biographical sources for Jesus are the four Gospels of the New Testament. Tacitus [55–120], Suetonius [75–160], and Josephus [37–100] are the first historians to refer to him, and they do so in an ambiguous way.) The only great religious leader whose existence is on firm historical ground is Mohammed (570–632).

The likelihood is that these religious innovators did really live but that a great many stories were added to the facts of their lives by other people. In their cases, the myth is thus a combination of historical fact and the special interpretations added to it later by those who set out to establish and disseminate their religious teachings.

An additional remark about the historicity of a religious myth. The fact that the historical foundation of a myth remains wrapped in mystery becomes the symbolic embodiment of the mystery with which the myth is concerned. For many people the mysterious is an essential quality of the religious experience. As we shall see in greater detail later, a myth generally deals with issues that are not tangible, verifiable, or easily limited in their meaning and consequences. In even the simplest religious myth at least some part remains obscure or beyond rational comprehension.

Myths like those of Abraham at the founding of Jewish history or of Jesus at the founding of Christianity have become powerful to the extent that they have deeply influenced and shaped the entire subsequent history of both the Jewish and the Christian world. The influence of myths, even religious ones, may extend beyond the groups to which they are immediately relevant, and this is the case with Abraham and Jesus.

A basic myth represents a special and fundamental approach to the eternal, or ever-recurring, issues of life. But not every such approach is expressed in the form of myth; nor does every approach that becomes a myth become a religious one. Socrates's life and death in ancient Greece had the profound effect and the grandeur of a myth, and certainly he touched on the eternal issues. Why did not Socrates's life become a myth? To be sure, his life and death were clearly documented by his contemporaries, especially Plato, so that there is no doubt whatsoever about his historical existence, and we do know many facts about the way he lived, thought, taught, and died. We have much more historical evidence about the terrestrial life of Socrates than we have about the life of Abraham and Moses, or even of Jesus Christ, who lived four centuries after Socrates. But none of the mystery of myth existed in the life of Socrates nor could it be fabricated. He never claimed special access to, or communication with, transcendental powers, although indeed he was a student of and a believer in them. Moreover, Socrates made an effort to remind himself and others of his human status and human limitations. "He knew only that he knew nothing." He never exceeded, or intended to exceed, the threshold of his human finitude; and so he remains a gigantic historical figure but not a mythical one.

Some historical events have an impact on the world or an immense, unforeseeable chain of effects similar to the great myths, and yet these events do not become myths. I shall mention a few of many possible examples. When Julius Caesar decided to cross that small river called the Rubicon, he knew that he was making an important, even a crucial decision, but the impact of that decision could not have been foreseen by him. He not only brought about a civil war against Pompey, but created the foundation of the Roman Empire. His act transformed the entire history of the ancient world and, indirectly, every subsequent era. Historians today are still interpreting the significance of the crossing of that miniscule river.

When a small group of men which included Benjamin Franklin, George Washington, John Adams, Thomas Jefferson, John Jay, Alexander Hamilton, James Wilson, and Thomas Paine planned the American Revolution and the writing of the American Constitution, they knew the importance of becoming independent from England. They could not be aware, however, of the profound political and cultural influence that the United States would eventually have on the international political scene.

But both Caesar and the Founding Fathers remain figures in the realm of the political and the temporal. We cannot call them mythical or mystical.

Perhaps closer to being mythical is the statement said to have been made by Galileo at the conclusion of the trial during which he recanted all beliefs and writings that held the sun to be the central body of the solar system. He said, *"Eppur si muove."* ("And yet it [the earth] moves.") With this sentence he reaffirmed that in his inner self he could not accept the beliefs being imposed on him, and that eventually science would confirm, beyond the possibility of controversy and to the whole world, the truth of his findings. Despite having recanted, Galileo towers as a giant. In spite of the fact that there is no historical documentation for Galileo having actually uttered the famous phrase, the story did not become a myth because: (1) it concerns a truth that was soon accepted by the whole of humanity without being wrapped in mystery; (2) science is limited to the immanent and does not deal with the transcendental.

We must now take into consideration two extremely important aspects of myths which run almost exactly counter to one another. The first, to which we have already referred, concerns the fact that great myths give a *decisive* and *specific* direction to a way of thinking and feeling and to an attitude toward the basic issues of life. The second is that they are *open-ended*, in some respects *indefinite* statements, *inexhaustible* sources of experience from which new leads are ever emerging. Let us examine both these aspects. In the first, the myth imparts a style of living or a fundamental characteristic to the people from which it springs. The Roman legend of Romulus and Remus is such a myth: the rearing of the twin brothers by a wolf and the aggressiveness, leading to the final victory of Romulus over

Remus, reveal the belligerent character of the Romans. The main characteristic as well as the chief virtue of Roman culture is military prowess. How different from the story of other brothers, or of twins, like mild Isaac and fierce Ishmael, or Jacob and Esau, where the wiser and gentler is the victor. Whereas the greatest Jewish book starts with the words "In the beginning God created the heavens and the earth," the greatest Latin book, *The Aeneid*, following the myth of Romulus and Remus, begins, *"Arma uirumque cano."* ("Of arms and the man I sing.") The man is Aeneas, a warrior. The myths of Romulus and Remus and of Aeneas, valid for the Romans, could not be acceptable to the Jews. Conversely, the myths surrounding Abraham, which came to represent and significantly to determine all subsequent Jewish history, were incomprehensible to the Romans.

Let us consider the second characteristic of the great myth, that it is an "open-ended" statement. Generally in any great myth we can find symbols of the whole human destiny, of man's challenge, groping, anguish, hope, illusion, tears, and anguish, defeat and triumph, sorrow and joy. The great myth takes us on an imaginative itinerary where, in spite of occasional pauses and suspense, we are aware, or at least half-aware, of a totality that is an echo of the cosmos, the human psyche, mankind, and whatever is beyond. The myth may be difficult to grasp, but in the end it will yield up some part of its meaning; for some glimpse of its truth will not evade us entirely. Its images may remain tenuous until the striking force of a new insight suddenly emerges and assails us. To be more specific, although the great myth deals with a presumably historical event, it must become plurivalent, and multidimensional, bespeaking values and issues that exist irrespective of time. Because it is an open statement, the great myth does not exhaust its power. Thus, although it may greatly diminish our hunger for basic truths, it never entirely satisfies us. Although each time we hear the story, we feel a sense of peace and contentment as the central insight is reaffirmed, we also feel a new urge to go further, a desire that the story may one day tell us even more.

A confrontation with a great myth is similar in a way to a confrontation with a great work of art: both can be evaluated each time with either a new insight or a new sense of appreciation. But whereas the fresh experience of a work of art pertains to, or is predominantly concerned with, problems of aesthetics, confrontation with the great myth primarily concerns ideals of human behavior or ethics or whatever relates to the transcendental, the metaphysical, the supernatural, or the divine. Although great religious myths and great works of art both produce in us deep experiences, the experiences are of different kinds. Content and form are important in both, but the work of art, as I said, provokes a response that is primarily aesthetic in which the evoked tension between the beautiful and the new truth ends in the victory of the beautiful; the great myth, if accepted, ends in the victory of a new or presumed new truth. Sounds, images and imaginery are in both; fantasy wedded to a realistic portrayal of the world is in both; but in the myth the message provides a norm for life. In other words, whatever truth is in the myth is contained not mainly in its aesthetic order or representation but in its concept—generally a concept that deals with the holy or the transcendental. Thus although the great myth may have great artistic value, its conceptual part counts most, even when this conceptual part is expressed more through fantasy and imaginative form than through pure logic and reason. The content of a great myth, like the content of a work of art, especially a literary work, quite often treats with some kind of disorder or tension or instability or all-out irrationality—which in turn reflects the disorder, tension, instability, or irrationality of mankind. And whereas the work of art often portrays the impossibility of solving the human predicament—and man is in a subtle way warned that he must resign himself to his unhappy lot —the religious myth, behind the tension, offers a prospect of peace or the hope for peace. In modern works of art, too, behind the disorder and the irrationality, we may eventually discover a hidden order. However, as I have already mentioned, whereas in the work of art the hidden order deals with the harmony of aesthetic forms, in the religious myth it deals with systems of ideas and an exaltation of the spirit that derive from the ideas. The work of art and the myth have other characteristics in common. Each is a totality, in spite of any arbitrary divisions in content. Both have structures that are solid even when not visible. In both there is a development that could not have been predicted, that goes against statistical probabilities, and that contrasts with the usual mechanical determinism of the world. Yet they differ crucially insofar as the religious myth aims at giving us specific spiritual guidance for daily life.

As we shall see in this book, the great myth accrues in meaning with the unfolding of human history. A back-and-forth exchange may occur: historical events can give new meaning to a myth, and the myth can throw light on historical events.

Finally, unless one takes the myth literally, the openness of the statement of the myth does not necessarily tie one who believes in it to a dogma. A person can remain ready to search without fear and to grow in the course of the search, and especially to find out more about oneself. A great myth can be viewed as a metaphorical expression of a truth, that is, a metaphysical metaphor. A myth is not a metaphor that deceives us or that takes us in because of its literary beauty; it is a metaphor that extends the vision of truth.

We can go deeper and deeper into the essence of a great myth, just as we can delve into the psyche of man. There is no end to the depth of man, no end to his mystery. Man, too, is a mythical figure—actually a myth. How can he be when we know for sure that he exists on this planet? We know that he exists, but we do not know him, or what we know of him for sure is nothing compared to the mystery he carries inside himself. He is not like a computer; No matter how complicated a computer is, it cannot become a man or a myth. Its complexity is explainable in function of the best-known part of its builder, the rationality of man.

We have compared a myth to a work of art. Can we compare a myth to a dream? In some respects, we can. Some psychoanalysts have interpreted myths as if they were dreams. The primitive mentality which Freud felt was ruled by that less-evolved organization of the mind called the primary process is found in both dreams and myths—and, I may add, in all products of creativity.* A dream reveals a truth in a fictitious way; a dream, too, is based on some segments of reality (the so-called residue of the day); but once a dream is interpreted or reported in words, it loses its nature and is no longer a dream. In other words, a dream cannot be experienced as a dream in any other way

* Silvano Arieti, *Creativity: The Magic Synthesis* (New York: Basic Books, 1979).

than in dream-form. The dream is a lived experience, and like the myth, is often lived more intensely than empirical reality. Nevertheless, when the dreamer wakes up, he rejects the dream as unreal, even if he gains some insights from it about his wishes and fears. Moreover, whatever insight he gains is for himself only. A myth is not so easily dismissed. Its meaning is not just for an individual, but extends to a group or to all mankind. A great myth is the result not only of primitive mentality or primary process cognition, but also of a harmonious fusion of primitive thinking and the highest levels of the mind.* At this point it is important also to consider whether psychoanalytic interpretation of myths must concern us here. Certainly psychoanalytic interpretations add new dimensions to our understanding. In some cases we may even accept an orthodox Freudian approach and recognize that the myth has something to do with such things as repressed sexuality, Oedipus complex, hatred for father, and so forth. To the extent that a myth is only of psychoanalytic interest, however, and does not transcend its original motivation, it will not be of major concern to us here. Even if the development of the myth that we are studying can be interpreted psychoanalytically as a form of sublimation, displacement, denial, and so forth, our interest will remain in the ultimate value of the myth at the highest levels of the psyche.

Some important issues remain to be considered. Given the fact that a myth can be representative of a basic approach to life, do we really need the myth as a medium for this approach? Several contemporary theologians and philosophers have posited the question of whether it is possible to demythologize religion. Some, like the theologian Ru-

* Ibid.

dolph Bultmann, think that it is, and should be possible. I myself believe that it is *theoretically* possible to demythologize religion, but I have no certain answer whether it would be desirable to do so. I am inclined to believe that to demythologize religion would not be advisable. For thousands of years great myths have served as tangible expressions of the intangible. They have given conceptual forms to what might otherwise have remained inconceivable. One thing, however, is certain. A system of religious beliefs should not rely only on myths for the understanding of life or for the application to life of whatever truth that system dispenses. The great myth must be understood as a starter, a springboard, a source of inspiration, comfort, and renewed search. This role is an immense endowment, but by itself is not enough to constitute the basic structure of a great religion.

Another issue, for which there is no clear-cut answer, is that of our ability to distinguish a valuable myth from one that promotes false or pernicious values. Unless making the distinction is left to an act of faith, it will be made by means of the individual's inner resources or, in the long run, by history.

In conclusion, it matters little whether a man by the name of Abraham really existed three or four thousand years ago in the Near East. Someone else may have existed who was similarly inspired at the beginning of the Hebrew history, or a group of people may collectively have formulated the concepts and events attributed to Abraham. But if we do accept as valid the feelings, the inspirations or revelations, the spiritual revolution generally connected with the name of Abraham—namely, the emergence of the idea of monotheism, the separation of spirit from matter—and if we do consider these events as a leap beyond some primordial stage of humanity and a metaphysical movement toward modernity, then we do accept Abraham. The name Abraham means all this and much more, as we shall see in subsequent chapters. This book is an attempt not so much to translate the language of an ancient myth into the language of the twentieth century but to evaluate the myth's relevance, in the past and in the contemporary world. In tackling so arduous a task, I am aware of how incomplete its results must be, not only because of my own limitations, but also because, as I have already said, the totality of the meaning of a great myth is always beyond human grasp. Even when exegesis, philosophy, theology, anthropology, psychology, and psychoanalysis join forces, only partial insights can be obtained. Apparently, the great myth is needed as a myth, and after bestowing whatever it has to offer, it remains a myth.

DUALISM

With his intuition (or revelation) of an incorporeal God separate from nature, Abraham divides spirit from matter. The repercussions of that decisive event have been felt by everyone who to one extent or another has come under the influence of Judeo-Christian civilization and of Western culture.

The intuition makes Abraham a dualist. He now divides what is accessible to (or conceived by) human beings into the physical and the spiritual. The term *dualism* is not agreeable to many people today; they prefer to consider everything that exists in a *monistic* frame of reference. According to the monists, there is no basic difference between mind and organism, psyche and soma, soul and body, the psychological and the physical, being and appearance, God and nature, and so on. As a matter of fact, Descartes has now become the common target of many philosophical arrows. Because of his basic formula *"Cogito ergo sum"* (I think, therefore I am"), and whatever is implied by it, Descartes is seen as an advocate of the duality of the universe. He is reputed to be the one who has plagued the modern world with dualism. In Hannah Arendt's last work, published posthumously,* the philosopher advocates a reversal of Descartes's metaphysical hierarchy by asserting that what counts or what really is, is only appearance. According to my understanding, she sees the world as a monistic complex of appearances.

If a dualistic approach is wrong, poor Descartes is at least innocent of having been the first to promulgate it. The problem goes back to Abraham. But let us see how wrong this dualistic approach really is.

Before doing so, however, I must take the reader as my companion on a brief journey into philosophical, neurophysiological, and psychiatric territory. I have already prepared the way for this unusual excursion by observing that a great myth is an open statement and that therefore we cannot predict in what directions it will take us; yet the reader by now probably nevertheless expects that we will remain in the religious or biblical realm. And, indeed, all the remaining chapters of this book will deal directly with the biblical story. But Abraham's great intuition, in my opinion, requires us to inquire into the recently controversial issue of dualism.

Another paradox may have struck the reader. From what I have said, one may have surmised that in my acceptance

* Hannah Arendt, *The Life of the Mind*, vol. 1: *Thinking* (New York: Harcourt, Brace, Jovanovich, 1977–78).

of the value of the myth I have been very much influenced by the eighteenth-century philosopher Giambattista Vico —in my opinion, a precursor of psychoanalysis and an early investigator of that part of the mental organization which Freud attributes to the primary process.* Yet Vico in his time fought Descartes's ideas vigorously. In certain respects the opposite of Vico, Descartes stresses the distinction between what he calls clear, distinct ideas (which Freud would later attribute to the secondary process) and that which exists in the mind as confused, vague, doubtful, fantasylike. According to Descartes, all things (and with no trace of doubt, only those) that we conceive clearly and distinctly are true. In the development of philosophy people who accept Descartes's orientation are anti-Vichian and vice versa: those who accept Vico's orientation are not Cartesians. Yet I, who consider myself fundamentally a Vichian in interpreting and attributing value to myths, become a Cartesian in accepting a dualistic orientation. My dualism, however, and the interactionism that follows from it stem not from Descartes but from more ancient roots—from Abraham.

Whatever the reason, there is no doubt that a monistic vision of the world, with no separation between mind and matter, is found by many people to be more appealing. Perhaps a monistic vision finds resonance in our aesthetic sense, which always responds more to a perception of uniy, no matter what we are considering. Perhaps monism appeals to our desire to interpret the entire universe in one way, supposedly the right one, and to dispense with any apparent mysticism. I myself find that, for reasons I have not totally elucidated but probably have to do with my

---

* Silvano Arieti, "Vico and Modern Psychiatry," in *Social Research* (1976) 43: 739–52.

scientific biological training, I would be inclined to prefer monism. But contrary to the majority of those inclined to monism, I feel we are not in a position to be so. In my view, all attempts to overcome dualism have failed, and dualism is inescapable. We have confused our state of understanding with our wishes. People who disdainfully refer to Descartes's explanation of the separation of mind and body as a bifurcation of nature believe that only matter, or disguised matter, exists. At other times, in a similarly derogatory manner, these people write that Descartes has placed a ghost (the soul) in the machine (the body). Actually it is to the merit of Descartes to have recognized that the problem of matter-spirit, or body-soul, can be visualized as a problem of brain-mind. The same problem could be referred to in different ways, according to the terminologies used or the particular aspect of the problem one wishes to focus on, as below:

nature-God
matter-spirit
body-soul
brain-mind
not-self–self
appearance-essence
deterministic causality-teleologic causality
physical pathology-psychopathology
monothetic-idiopathic
cosmic-historical
explanation-understanding

MAN CREATED IN THE IMAGE OF GOD

Returning to Abraham: when he "saw" the incorporeality of God, who was separate from matter, did he initiate the Hebrew tradition that man was created in the image of

God? I believe he did. Since Abraham's conception of God is that of an incorporeal and imageless being, the expression "created in the image of God" must not be taken literally. It must refer to the spiritual (or psychological) part of the human being. Whereas God as conceived by Abraham may be all spiritual and incorporeal, man is not. He belongs to two worlds. He has a body, from which the spiritual and psychological emerge. Thus any theology that affirms that man was created in the image of God implies a dualism in the human state: body and psyche. Since God is incorporeal, the image of God must be reflected in the psyche.

Although there are disagreements on this crucial issue, we could say that man reflects to some extent the image of God insofar as:

1. He is able to understand: that is, that he is able not only to make contacts with the present but also to infer the absent and to be conscious of himself.
2. He has the capacity to distinguish good from evil.
3. He has the capacity to choose (or will).
4. He has the capacity to love.
5. He has the capacity to create.

These five characteristics can be considered psychological activities of the mind or even functions mediated by the brain. One can even go so far as to say that rudiments of these activities can be found in subhuman animals. As a matter of fact, between subhuman animals and Homo sapiens there are quantitative differences that are possibly explainable by Darwinian theory. But even if it is so, we cannot disregard the fact, which I shall discuss at greater length later, that quantitative differences can bring about qualitative differences that change the essence of the animal: it is no longer just an animal but a human being as well. Certain functions, as they appear in low animal forms, can be viewed as being only physiological or neurological; in higher animal forms they may be considered as psychological, and in human beings as spiritual.

Let us examine these five characteristics separately.

1. *Capacity to understand*. Animals have a certain capacity to understand the environment, a capacity that relies on the immediately given, that is, on what the animal receives from its perceptions of the external world. The animal's mentality is restricted to what it sees, hears, smells, touches, as well as to the demands or needs of its body, like hunger, thirst, and sexual desire. An animal's mentality also governs its instinctive, or reflex, responses to its sensations, perceptions, and needs. An animal can elaborate only minimally on the data offered by its perceptions and needs. It is compelled to live in the present. Many species may also respond to something that is absent, but only if they perceive some sign that the something is about to become present, or is actually present but hidden—for example, food that cannot be seen but can be smelled. We can say that animals are motivated by physiological wishes—for instance, by the wish to eat, to drink, and to copulate; but these wishes are better called appetites.

One should not confuse such animal wishes with what humans experience as desires. A desire is a wish for what is not present, for what one would like to have present or would like to own. The elementary animal functions expand enormously in the human being and undergo transformations that give them a different scope, one not recognizable in the nonhuman. In the human mind, the perceptions of the senses are elaborated, making abstractions from the elementary sense data. These abstractions involve not only what is present but also what is absent; not only what is here, but also what could in probability or in theory be here, now and in the future. The human being develops systems of symbolism—like imagery, language, mathematics—through which he can indefinitely expand not only what he receives from the external world but also whatever he can conjecture. The human mind, although in need of external stimuli, is not tied to them. In addition to symbolic and abstract thinking, the human being is given another important function (still to be included under the heading of understanding): self-consciousness. The human being is not only conscious, but he is also conscious of being conscious. As far as we know or can deduce from the findings of comparative psychology, animals are not self-conscious. By anthropomorphizing we can say, for instance, that a dog has a special type of personality, but we cannot say it has a self. A dog is not able to abstract itself from its organism to observe itself as others would observe it.* A human being can also be conscious of the limitations of his knowledge. By being conscious of himself, the human being achieves the status of being a unity, a sentient and self-understanding unity, separate from whatever exists in the world. And in this respect we may find a similarity between the human being and the image of God.

2. *Capacity to distinguish good and evil.* We enter here into a different system of categories, which also permits us to see man in the image of God. For man, too, is able to distinguish good and evil.

---

* Some philosophers deny this faculty to man, too. According to Kant, the mind is always a subject (a knower) and never the object of knowledge. However, Kant, too, speaks of a "synthetic unity of apperceptions and of a transcendental unity"; we really do not know to what extent Kant denies a self, a person who knows himself and knows of knowing himself.

In the biblical myth, human beings acquire the capacity to distinguish good and evil when the first couple, Adam and Eve, appear on earth. This is tantamount to saying that in order to be a human being, rather than prehuman, a man or a woman must have acquired an ethical faculty. The human being must have the ability to evaluate whether an act is right or wrong—that is, whether it is good or bad.

3. *Capacity to choose and to will.* The human being is able not only to understand various possibilities open to him and to distinguish them under two ethical categories of good and evil, but he is also able to make a choice from among various options and to will, that is, to implement his chosen action. Since the choice is his, he is responsible for it. No longer is he a passive spectator, who has to undergo whatever is imposed on him; like God, although to an infinitesimally smaller degree, he becomes an initiator, a mover, an agent. He disrupts the deterministic order of the world and becomes free. In the cosmos known to us, freedom originates with the will of man. By choosing between good and evil, man not only exercises his capacity to understand and to will, but also uses his ability to attribute values—an ethical dimension—to his choices. By using his capacity to distinguish good and evil and to choose and will, the human being transcends every less-evolved form of life, and a system of values becomes an integral part of his existence. If we stress that man is an animal similar, say, to an ape or that he is only an evolved ape, we continue to classify man as an entity without morality—like a stone, an amoeba, or a tiger—unable to distinguish right from wrong. The human faculties that permit man to choose between right and wrong are derived from previous levels of evolution, but in man these faculties undergo a transmutation that adds an ethical dimension. By choos-

ing, a person to some extent makes himself. Thus the individual is the result not only of previous or present circumstances but also of his own choices—choices made throughout life. He is thus to a limited degree his own maker, and in this respect he is to a limited extent similar to God.

Man's capacity to choose between right and wrong does not, as some theorists imply, mean that he is born either bad or good. Rabbi Jack Bemporad says:

> Once we recognize that man is by nature neither good nor evil and that both his good and his evil are human qualities and that man has the freedom to actualize either good or evil, then we are able to recognize the traditional Jewish teaching with respect to the nature of man.
>
> It is important to note, however, that both the view that man is essentially good and that he is essentially evil have had negative social and historical consequences. If man is seen as essentially good, then it is believed that social progress comes about merely by taking away all those elements that impede the realization of this goodness. Thus, the social order is geared negatively. The philosophy of the Enlightenment clearly demonstrates this fact. If all that society must do is merely to prevent ignorance and maintain a "laissez-faire" attitude, since by giving man utmost freedom he will by nature realize goodness, then no real thought is given to social planning and to achieving the task of realizing the spiritual potential within man. . . .
>
> If, on the other hand, one assumes that man is by nature evil, then social planning again becomes useless since man by his nature can only bring about evil and needs some external power or leader graced by God to bring about social cohesiveness. This makes man excessively passive and puts him at the mercy of an authoritarian type society.*

* Jack Bemporad, "The Concept of Man after Auschwitz," in *Out of the Whirlwind* (Union of American Hebrew Congregations, 1968), pp. 477–87.

4. *Capacity to love.* Love is not the desire for possession. It presupposes a capacity to choose and to value. The happiness and well-being of the object of our love is as important to us as our own happiness and well-being. In love I give, and in love I receive. In love I distinguish the object of my love from myself and yet at the same time establish the strongest possible bond with the one I love. Human beings in their conception of God, have given prominence to His love for humanity. Love becomes one of the highest values, the value that we generally choose over every other value. I shall have much more to say on this topic in chapter 2.

5. *Capacity to create.* Like God, man creates. However, man's *creativi*ty is different from God's creation. God creates from nothingness, *ex nihilo*, as theologians say, whereas man creates from what he has available to him, from what is given to him by others, by nature, and by his own intellectual powers. He recombines what is present, and thus makes new forms. Just as to some extent he is the creator of himself by virtue of the choices he makes, he becomes the maker of creative products by using his powers of abstraction, symbolization, and insight. He becomes a partner of God in the act of creation, in the act of actualizing part of the infinite possibility of the universe.

THE PHILOSOPHICAL APPROACH

These five capacities of man which suggest that he is made in the image of God are attributed by most philosophical and theological schools to the soul or to the mind. Can the concept of soul or mind be considered in a dualistic or in a monistic frame of reference? Entire libraries have been written about the problem, but it will suffice to take a kind of bird's-eye view of only the most important philosophical, psychiatric, and neuro-physiological theories as an introduction to the problem in the contemporary world.

According to Plato, the soul consists of immaterial substance. The soul and the body are intimately related, but there is a clear-cut distinction between them. The soul, originating in the supersensible world of eternal Forms or Ideas, is not comfortable in its interactions with matter and eventually returns to the realm of the eternal. For Aristotle the soul is the life principle, the organization of the processes of living, or the sum of these processes.

A new era begins with Descartes. Soul as such is mentioned less and less, and mind takes its place. Descartes finds in the human mind first of all a way to remove doubts. *"Cogito, ergo sum"*—"I think, therefore I am." The fact that I think is proof of my existence. There are two substances: the incorporeal—the mind, and the material. The mind resides in the brain. But the brain consists of two identical hemisphere. Since like the soul, the mind is indivisible, it must reside in a part of the brain that cannot be divided. That part, according to Descartes, is a little organ located over the third ventricle between the two hemispheres, the pineal gland. Descartes's basic dualism thus rests on the concepts of mind and brain.

Kant criticizes the traditional view of the mind as a substance, but speaks instead of a personal unity or self.

Hume cannot think of the mind as a separate entity. He also attacks the concept of the self—for him, a nonexistent entity. In the *Treatise of Human Nature* he writes:

> For my part, when I enter most intimately into what I call
> *myself*, I always stumble on some particular perception or
> other, of heat or cold, light or shade, love or hatred, pain
> or pleasure. I never can catch myself at any time without
> a perception, and never can observe anything but the
> perception.

Hume does not seem to attach importance to the fact that
very seldom do we perceive or become aware of things in
their entirety, and yet we may have a concept of them,
and be sure of their existence. For instance, I may be in
London, New York, or Rome and be aware only of my
surroundings. Yet I have the knowledge that I am on the
planet earth, and that the planet earth exists and consists
of many regions, including the cities of London, New
York, and Rome. Hume contradicts himself repeatedly, as
for instance, when he refers to himself as "I" and "myself,"
an entity which, according to him, does not exist.

For some philosophers, mind is only a form of behavior.
For Dewey * mind is intelligent behavior. For Gilbert
Ryle † there is no need to refer to the concept mind; we
should just stick to describing how people behave.

Some thinkers try to solve the problem of mind-body by
resorting to the concept of parallelism. Mental processes
and physical processes are both real, but not related. They
merely accompany each other. A thought of mine merely
accompanies a process that takes place in some neurons of
my brain. This concept of parallelism seems to me impossible to accept. At the same time that it reaffirms the existence of the two realms (brain and psyche) and the fact

---

* John Dewey, *The Quest for Certainty* (New York: Putnam, 1929).
† Gilbert Ryle, *The Concept of Mind* (New York: Barnes & Noble,
1949).

of their coexistence, the concept does not explain why the two realms should always be together and run parallel.

Other thinkers attribute to the mind the role of an epiphenomenon. To them, whatever is mental is a by-product —an accidental function—of the organ called brain. It is hard to see how the highly purposive, complicated, and potentially ever more complex functions of the human mind can be relegated to the role of an epiphenomenon.

Just as epiphenomenalism rejects the phenomenon mind as a fundamental entity, the school of psychic monism accepts only the mind and rejects everything else. The body (including the brain) is merely an appearance. When we believe the body exists, we are victims of a pathetically naive realism. Although I find myself drawn to certain concepts of the idealistic school, I cannot conceive of a monism that totally denies the existence of an external reality.

PSYCHIATRIC, PSYCHOLOGICAL, AND PSYCHOANALYTIC APPROACHES

I believe that the problem of mind-brain is pertinent to the fields of psychiatry, psychology, psychoanalysis, and neurophysiology and that people working in these fields can play an important role in the attempt to find new formulations and clarifications of this problem.

The psychological school of behaviorism believes that it has found the solution to the problem by accepting materialistic monism. There is no such thing as mind; there is only the behavior of a living physical organism. Other schools of psychology and psychiatry recognize that the problem is not so simple. They advocate various compromises, which, however, tend more to obfuscate the issue than to clarify it. According to official medical science and within the medical schools, the brain and the mind have been associated for a long time. Until a few decades ago in many medical schools the functions and the diseases of both the brain and the psyche were studied and taught in one department of neuro-psychiatry. But the hyphen between neuro and psychiatry could hardly disguise the split between neurology (the study of the functions and diseases of the nervous system) and psychiatry (the study of the functions and diseases of the psyche). Although it is never denied that psychological functions and dysfunctions are directly connected with the brain, these functions and dysfunctions are recognized as having characteristics of their own, completely different from neurological characteristics. Ultimately, mastering both neurology and psychiatry became too difficult for one person, and generally a physician had to decide to specialize in only one of the fields.

In most medical schools, however, the so-called neuro-psychiatric approach, which was founded by the German physician Wilhelm Griesinger, remained prominent for a long time, both in Europe and in the United States. What happened actually where Griesinger's notion held sway was that so-called neuro-psychiatry became a part of neurology. As a result a monistic, materialistic approach prevailed, and psychiatric disorders came to be interpreted as disorders of the brain, or as a category of neurological diseases. Since no anatomical alterations could be found by either gross or microscopic inspection in such conditions as manic-depressive psychosis, schizophrenia, depression, paranoia and paranoid states, and psychoneuroses, the view was repeatedly expressed that these conditions were based on metabolic or biochemical disorders. This view prevailed until the Second World War, and reacquired prominence again later, as we shall see.

But at the beginning of the Second World War psychoanalysis and psychodynamic psychiatry in the United States began to play a kind of role that they had failed to achieve in earlier decades. In treating psychiatric conditions great importance came to be given to factors originating in the psyche and to the influence of the external environment on the psyche of the individual throughout his life history. The brain was relegated to a secondary role, although it was never denied that the brain was always involved in psychiatric conditions. However, such conditions were considered "functional," that is, mediated by *the functions* of the brain, not caused by anatomical alterations. How the brain "mediated" these conditions was never clarified.

From Freud to present day, psychoanalysts and psychodynamic psychiatrists have found only unsuccessful compromises to explain the phenomenon. Although Freud more than any other psychiatrist elucidates the nature of man's psychological functions—the functions of the mind—philosophically he considers himself a materialist, and he adheres to a materialistic monism. Yet when with a superb force of expression he writes of "the mysterious leap from psyche to soma" in recognition that some psychological conditions can produce anatomical disorders, he instantly reaffirms the existence of the psyche and the soma as two different entities and indicates the mystery of the interaction between the two. Many other psychiatrists speak of the mysterious leap in the other direction—from soma to psyche—to indicate that anatomical alterations produce alterations of the psychological functions. Of course the most popular attempt to reunite the soma and the psyche is in psychosomatic medicine. But whether we speak of something as being psychosomatic (that is, both psychological and bodily) or of the "mysterious leap," we reaffirm the existence of the two components, the psyche and the soma. In the attempt to deny dualism we reaffirm it.

Lately some branches of psychiatry (but not necessarily of neuro-physiology as we shall see) have tried to obviate the problem by fully embracing a biological, materialistic frame of reference. In the last ten to fifteen years many psychiatrists have returned to the original Griesinger-Kraepelin concepts that all alterations of the psyche are fundamentally organic. Even though the recent introduction of the electromicroscope has failed to reveal anatomical alterations of the brain in conditions like schizophrenia, manic-depressive psychosis, and psychoneuroses, many people uphold the belief that the abnormality is based on molecular or biochemical alterations not visible by means of the methods currently available. In this view, psychological factors play no role or only a minimal one.

In my opinion it is impossible to deny that chemical substances can alter the functions of the brain or that the psychological activities of the brain are accompanied by chemical phenomena. However, it is also impossible to deny that the human brain is constituted so as to enable the individual to face the psychological challenges of life. The brain offers to the human being the possibility of dealing with the world and with himself in psychological ways. But what are these psychological ways? Even if they need biochemical mechanisms in order to take place, they seem to be much more than chemical reactions.

EMERGENT EVOLUTION
AND INTERACTIONISM

I believe that we can make some progress in studying the relation between soma and psyche by adopting the concepts of emergent evolution and of interactionism, as expressed by some philosophers, biologists, psychiatrists, and contemporary neuro-physiologists.

To my knowledge, C. Lloyd Morgan * first introduced the theory of emergence in a philosophical context. According to Morgan, new forms periodically appear in the universe which cannot be explained by reference to previously existing forms. Higher levels of evolutionary forms are brought about by the addition of elements; these higher levels are more than mere regroupings of elements already present. These additions are innovative and unpredictable. We know empirically that by combining two gases in a certain proportion (hydrogen and oxygen) we obtain water. But could an astronomer, observing our world from a totally different universe, predict that the marvelous fluid, water, would emerge from the combination of two gases? Or could even inhabitants of this planet explain why, from a specific combination of hydrogen and oxygen, water emerges?

Similarly, we know that the human brain is anatomically and physiologically related in the phyletic scale to the brain of other primates and of all mammals and of all vertebrates. But were we astronomers on another solar system studying the phenomena on earth, could we predict that a few million added neurons would transform the brain of a

---

* C. Lloyd Morgan, *Emergent Evolution* (New York: Holt, 1923).

35

chimpanzee into the brain of a human being, who thus becomes able to talk, to think abstractly, to have self-consciousness, to distinguish right from wrong and good from evil, to be capable of choosing, willing, loving, and creating? In other words, is it possible to predict (or explain why) the enlargement of the cerebral cortex has made possible the *emergence* of those characteristics that permit us to see man as made in the image of God? The answer is no. Even if a special enlargement of the cerebral cortex is necessary to bring about the emergence of these psychological (or soul-like) faculties, it is undeniable that these faculties have emerged, that is, have appeared during a certain period of time in the history of the world.

Morgan states that there is no mind without life; and no life without some physical basis. For him, "Life stands to matter in the same kind of relation as mind stands to life." In his view, emergent evolution explains all the "upward" changes that have accrued in the history of our cosmos, from the atom (now we say from subatomic structures) to the mind of man. For Morgan, nature is still in the making and follows an "orderly constructiveness." *He does not explain, however, the origin of this orderly constructiveness.*

He writes:

Emergent evolution works upwards from matter, through life, to consciousness which attains in man its highest reflective or super-reflective level. It accepts the "more" at each ascending stage as that which is given, and accepts it to the full. The most subtle appreciation of the artist or the poet, the highest aspiration of the saint, are no less accepted than the blossom of the water lily, the crystalline fabric of a snowflake, or the minute structure of the atom.

Emergent evolution urges that the "more" of any given stage, even the highest, involves the "less" of the stages which were precedent to it and continue to coexist with it. It does *not* interpret the higher in terms of the lower only; for that would imply denial of the emergence of those new modes of natural relatedness which characterize the higher and make it what it is. Nor does it interpret the lower in terms of the higher.

How do these emergences come about? According to Morgan, there is a *nisus* (a creative synthesis) that discloses a purpose (a direction toward higher forms) inherent in nature. One must also hypothesize a vast cosmic tendency and the creative and determining power of God. For Morgan this power is immanent in whatever is created, and not transcendent.

Other points of view, more modern than those of Morgan, see the unfolding of the phyletic scale in biological evolution as based to a large extent on mutations. The emergences are mutations, or inaccuracies, in the hereditary constitution, consisting of the addition of a new chromosome, the loss of a chromosome, or some change within a chromosome. When mutations occur, new gamuts of spontaneity unfold, that is, a range of new possibilities presents itself. Most mutations are unfavorable as far as survival is concerned. They make adaptation very difficult and may lead to the extinction of the species. But an extremely small number of mutations *are* favorable, if they happen to occur when improbable environmental situations have also developed which enhance their survival and enable them to compete successfully with nonmutant forms. Evolution is seen as the result of the sequence of the favorable mutations which have changed the organism and made it more complex and capable of competing successfully with the nonmutant species.

In the psyche of man, we can attribute to emergent evo-

lution those qualities that enable us to view the human being as created in the image of God, and therefore as having
a soul—namely, symbolism, self-reflection, an ethical sense,
the capacity to choose, to will, to love, and to create. If
we believe in God, we may believe that God resorted to
biological evolution to install these faculties in the human
being. What Abraham saw in God was the absolute forms
of these qualities. However, this complicated matter cannot be seen so simply on at least two counts. God, resorting to emergent evolution at a certain point in history in
order to endow man with soul-like qualities, would really
seem to be playing the role of a Greek *deus ex machina*.
Both the existence and the interventions of God must be
inferred in other ways. Let us examine again the Darwinian
theories and their derivatives. They explain the hierarchy,
the passage from lower to higher forms in the ways described above. Mutations that occur by chance, combined
with the selection of the fittest, produce order—a systema-
tic order of increasing complexity, from the amoeba to man.
Over a length of time even the most improbable mutant
combinations occur by chance in an environment where at
that particular moment they happen to be the fittest.

Let us assume that all this is correct, and I believe that
it is. An important element is still missing: the mystery of
the potentiality for order—what Morgan calls orderly constructiveness. Where does the potentiality for order come
from? How does the magic synthesis occur? If the highest
levels of organization exist as a possibility, they must exist
somewhere that transcends the immanent. The existence of
this possibility is necessary beyond any combination of mutations and chance. The potentiality for something not inherent in matter cannot be called immanent. My views are
close to Morgan's, but I feel that his concept of *nisus*, al-

though it is an advance over previous theories, is not sufficient.

Why are some light waves, upon reaching the human retina, transformed into sensations of red, green, and other colors? Why do we laugh when we hear something humorous, blush when we are embarrassed, yawn when we are bored?

In most instances we are able to describe phenomena that come under our observation and even to discover new relations—that is, associations among phenomena; but we are not able satisfactorily to explain the mysterious transformation of the physical into the mental, or the mental into the physical. Similarly, we are not able to explain in purely physical terms the formation of orderly constructiveness.

Ludwig von Bertalanffy, a biologist competent in many related fields, a man whom I greatly respected and admired, and to whom I was bound by personal friendship, tries to get around the problem of dualism with a new science that is to a large extent the result of his own creativity. Known as the general systems theory, it tries to recognize structural similarities, or isomorphies, in different fields. Such unrelated fields as statistics, literature, psychology, and social problems follow certain identical principles or laws. When entities of any kind—physical, mathematical or mental—are considered together, they form systems and are subject to laws discovered and formulated by general systems theory.*,† To paraphrase Laszlo,‡ whereas science,

---

* Ludwig von Bertalanffy, "General Systems Theory," *Main Currents in Modern Thought* 11 (1955) 75–83.

† Ludwig von Bertalanffy, *General Systems Theory* (New York: Braziller, 1969).

‡ Ervin Laszlo, *The Systems View of the World* (New York: Braziller, 1972).

at least Newtonian science, deals with organized simplicity, general systems theory deals with organized complexities: the complexities of systems. Systems or wholes or ensembles are not just things; they are groups of interacting parts that maintain certain relationships among themselves. By putting together fields pertaining to the physical universe and others pertaining to the mental world, and by successfully abstracting common principles, one might imagine that the dualistic barrier had been overcome. I do not believe, however, that such is the case. I once asked the following question of von Bertalanffy: "You have been able to discover and differentiate these universal laws, or general principles. It is a tremendous accomplishment. But where do these principles come from? Why, when entities are together, do systems and principles which rule these principles emerge?" Von Bertalanffy said he could not give me an answer. If I understood him correctly, he rejects the idea that systems are an invention of our mind. Systems, that is, the orders of things, exist, but why they exist or where they come from we do not know.

In my view, no matter what groupings we consider, we can always abstract from them a transcendental principle of order.

Many people who accept emergent evolution continue nevertheless to see it as a phenomenon exclusively explicable in a monistic biological or a material frame of reference. Recently, however, support for a dualistic and interactionist approach has come from an unexpected source: a group of eminent scientists. A number of prominent contemporary neuro-physiologists who have studied the human brain for most of their lives have become more daring than many psychiatrists and psychologists in denouncing the notion of physical monism and in concluding that the dualism of our world is inescapable. According to the scientists, the only avenue open to contemporary neurophysiology and psychology is to accept interactionism—that is, the theory of an interaction between psyche and brain. The Nobel Prize winner John E. Eccles, one of the leading neuro-physiologists of our time, believes that dualism and interactionism are evident. In the human being who thinks, feels, assesses ethically, chooses, wills, and loves, neural events do occur, but the human's thoughts, feelings, evaluations, choices, and actions are different from the neural events by which they are produced. No "identity theory" is tenable which equates physical events like molecular, biochemical, or electrical phenomena with the psychological events to which they are causally related. Patterns of neuronal activities are functional units from which some psychological events emerge. One of these emerging mental events is consciousness, which takes place in both cerebral hemispheres; other mentals events—consciousness of being conscious and self-consciousness—seem to emerge only in the left cerebral hemisphere. These mental events in their turn exert an influence on neuro-physiological events.

Dualism and interaction are also reaffirmed by R. W. Sperry, a neuro-physiologist who has made epoch-making breakthroughs in his studies of the right cerebral hemisphere. And from other fields, the philosopher Karl Popper and the historian of psychology Walter B. Weiner have joined the party of the interactionists.

On the other hand, a majority of even the psychiatrists who are interested in psychosomatic medicine limit themselves to describing how psychological factors, mediated through the autonomic nervous system, bring about physical conditions like gastric ulcers, hypertension, and asthma. They have bypassed the involvement of the central nervous system. Few of them have dared to oppose the prevailing positivist and monistic approach. This lack of courage prompted R. W. Sperry to write in 1976:

> When I initially stated this view in 1965 [namely, the view that mental events can cause neuro-physiological events], one had to search a long way in philosophy, and especially in science, to find anyone who would put into writing that mental forces or events are capable of causing physical changes in an organism's behavior or its neurophysiology. With rare exceptions writings in behavioral science dealing with perception, imagery, emotion, cognition, and various other mental phenomena were very cautiously phrased to conform with prevailing materialist-behaviorist doctrine. Care was taken to be sure that the subjective phenomena should not be implied to be more than passive correlates or inner aspects of brain events, and especially to avoid any implication that the mental phenomena might interact causally with physical brain process.*

Indeed, I myself can provide special confirmation for Sperry's claim: when in papers written during the 1950s and the 1960s I made this point, no one (including, I may say, Sperry himself) took it up or even responded.

FROM DUALISM TO SANCTIFICATION

Before returning to Abraham, we must extend our excursion for just a bit longer. Let us first briefly reconsider the basic characteristics that emerge in the human being and confer on him the qualities of soul. We have already con-

---

* R. W. Sperry, "Mental Phenomena as Causal Determinants in Brain Functions," in G. G. Globus, G. Maxwell, and I. Savodnik (eds.), *Consciousness and the Brain* (New York: Plenum, 1976).

sidered them in a somewhat cavalier fashion in the categories of emergent mutation; now they deserve deeper consideration. These characteristics are revolutionary; their emergence is so significant that by comparison the Copernican is a dwarf revolution. As we have seen, animals too have a certain kind of sensitivity and consciousness (vastly advancing them beyond non-animal forms), but the human being is the first entity to become self-conscious, or to be conscious of being conscious. With Descartes, man can say, "*Cogito ergo sum.*" Even if this statement is wrong, man's being able to make such a statement is of critical significance. The statement implies dualism: "I am, but something else other than myself—extended and external—is there."

With his symbolic powers, the human being can conceive that which is absent from his immediate perceptions, in the past, the present, and the future. Moreover, whatever the human being observes is either an action of his own or an event, like the fall of a leaf, to which he attributes value: he judges the action or event from the point of view of its being beautiful or ugly, desirable or undesirable, good or bad, right or wrong. Most important, in a deterministic world where everything is the result of previous causes, the human being emerges as the exception, one who retains some freedom, who has a margin of will. Sartre, who —at least in the beginning of his philosophical journey— was a Cartesian, believed in dualism and in the fact that man is free. Nevertheless, he maintained that there is no God or transcendental order. For Sartre, man himself is the king and the sovereign of himself.

For myself, it is impossible to accept freedom and dualism without the conception of transcendental order. This transcending order may or may not be conceived as God or as an Ultimate Cause and Order.

The dualism that divides, or abstracts, mind from body, the inner from the external world, the private, idiographic, and subjective from the shared, nomothetic, and objective, the historical from the cosmic, order from disorder, system from the haphazard play of the accidental, what is known by acquaintance from what is known by description —this dualism finds its first expression in Abraham's separation of God from nature. What is implied by this dualism is an ultimate principle that transcends the physical, even if the manifestations of this principle are required to interact with the physical. Even if the mental is required to arise from the physical, it goes beyond the physical and bespeaks something that comes before and after the physical. Only man is able to receive by intuition or revelation the existence of this ultimate principle; and because of this ability, he can be conceived as being made in the image of God. To accept Abraham's dualism and interactionism means also to accept the interaction between God and the world, God and the human being. God and the human being act upon each other, as is testified in the biblical account of Abraham, to be described in chapters 3 and 4.

Of course, there are different ways of reacting to Abraham's dualism and interactionism. Christianity, for example —especially in the Middle Ages, but to some extent until recent times—has preached contempt for the physical world and the body and stressed the psychological, the spiritual, and the immortal soul. Saul of Tarsus, later to call himself Paul, considers the body as an impediment to the requirements of the spirit and as the source of many evils. According to Paul, sexual desire is undesirable, and he advises unmarried men to stay away from women. He sees any carnal pleasure, especially sexual pleasure, as something that does not permit man spiritual purity. Four centuries later, Augustine reaffirms this teaching. Christianity, then, is dualistic, but within its dualism only the spiritual counts and has eternal value. On the other hand, it is on the actual incarnation of the divine, in the body of Jesus, that the religion is founded. The physical and the spiritual attain their perfect, and their only possible perfect, union in Jesus Christ, God, and man at the same time.

This concept has always been unacceptable to the Jews, who conceive—as Abraham does—the one incorporeal, invisible, all and always spiritual God. According to the Jewish view, the idea of divine incarnation is a concession—though, to be sure, in only one instance—to the pagan tendency to see the divine in human forms.

That this view of God as assuming human form has not been alien to the Christian tradition, in spite of the fact that Christianity, like Judaism, stresses the incorporeal and spiritual essence of God, is demonstrated in Christian literature and art through the centuries, in ways inconceivable to the Hebrew tradition. Two examples will suffice. In Michelangelo's glorious ceiling in the Sistine Chapel, God Himself, in the act of creating Adam, is portrayed as a man, an elder with a long beard. And in one of the most salient passages of *The Divine Comedy*, the last and probably the most beautiful canto of the *Paradiso*, Dante describes the ultimate and final accomplishment of his mystic journey, the direct sight of God:

> O Light Eternal, who alone abidest in Thyself, alone knowest Thyself, and, known to Thyself and knowing, lovest and smilest on Thyself! That circling which, thus begotten, appeared in Thee as reflected light, when my eyes had dwelt on it for a time, seemed to me depicted with our image

within itself and in its own color, wherefore my sight was entirely set upon it.*

Thus, according to Dante, not only when Jesus Christ appears on earth but in heaven, too, the mystery of incarnation is repeated. God appears as a man (depicted with our image) or is a man, at the same time as He remains God.

The Jewish tradition, while maintaining that man was created in the image of God always refrains, even in art and poetry, from conceiving of God in any form of incarnation.

On the other hand, in the Jewish tradition from Abraham to our own day there is no contempt for the body; it is seen as part of life. Judaism recognizes that we cannot make all of our life spiritual, for that would be a return to a monism that is not possible in the condition of being human. What we can do is to sanctify our life with our actions by following the ways of God. While the Christian tradition focuses on the salvation of the soul, or on eternal life after the death of the body; in Jewish doctrine, life on earth counts, too, and what I as an individual do has an eternal effect not only on my soul but on earth as well. Thus the human being must strive to sanctify life. Reverence for life, as advocated by someone like Albert Schweitzer, is a wonderful thing, but it is not enough. Life must be *sanctified*. The Jewish concept of *Kedushah* refers to this sanctification. God alone is totally holy. In primitive Semitic religions the holy is considered a quality inherent in objects and idols and in nature. After Abraham, true holiness is confined to God, though it can be participated in by man to the degree that he sanctifies his earthly life by following in the ways of God. Such sanctification

* *Paradiso*, trans. C. S. Singleton (Princeton: Princeton University Press, 1975), canto 33, verses 124–32.

can be achieved not only through the acts of the individual but through those of the whole of mankind. Thus history may take, and ultimately will take, a redemptive course. The people of Israel can be sanctified if they abide by their Covenant with God. Eventually the whole world will be sanctified in the Messianic age, when, as the prophet Joel promised, the spirit of God will be poured on all flesh.* This notion of the sanctification of life is stressed in Jewish tradition throughout the centuries, though in a variety of ways. In relatively recent times the philosopher Moritz Lazarus, under the influence of neo-Kantian school, holds that one becomes holy through moral actions; in abiding by the categorical imperative, society is sanctified. For the philosopher Hermann Cohen, the holy resides in ethical activity, where the human and the divine meet.

Thus in the Jewish tradition the sanctification of life becomes the most desirable form of interaction between the divine and the human, between spirit and matter. Rather than accepting any form of monism, the human being must make a spiritual mark on his mortal existence by following what he feels is required of him and what he requires of himself. In so doing, man will integrate in the best possible way the two aspects of his human existence.

But if at a human level, sanctification of life is the most desirable form of dualism-interactionism, Jewish tradition also points to another form of interactionism at an even higher level: interactionism between God and history. God is not just in heaven, and those who communicate with Him are not fleeing from earth into a timeless and space-less infinity. And whereas God is wholly spiritual—and history can only be spiritual to a limited extent because

---

*Joel 3:1–2. In Christian translations of the Bible, this passage is generally indicated as 2:28.

human beings are involved in it—God is not indifferent to history. He always interacts with it. It is from within history that Abraham communicates with God, as do all the subsequent prophets. They hear His voice in the events of the day, they recognize His will, they see in earthly events not a random succession of facts but the unfolding of a process. This process cannot be uniformly directed toward goodness and higher goals, because the will of man takes part in it and interferes with its course.

Many philosophical conceptions of history are alien to the Jewish tradition. I shall briefly review the main ones. One, starting with Hesiod, typical of Greek culture, sees history as progressive decadence, going through five stages. From a golden age history progressively and ineluctably decays to a silver, a bronze, a heroic, and finally a human age. Hesiod's conception is alien to the Jewish spirit because it implies that fate is stronger than the divinity. This theory is an ancient way of applying to human history a principle that much later in science came to be called the second principle of thermodynamics (progressive entropy, or destruction of the universe). (See chapter 2, page 100.) The second theory interprets history as a cycle that ineluctably repeats itself. The ancient Stoic belief is that each cycle is identical to the previous one; more recent is Spengler's belief that the cycles are identical not in content but only in form or structure. Jewish tradition admits to a possible repetition of events, but again not in a preordained cycle. Compulsory repetition denies the unfolding of a process—denies the presence of God. And so does the third theory, which sees history as purely the result of chance or of random events. A fourth theory sees human history as progress but does not explain how progress comes about. A fifth theory sees history as the affirmation of a progress that is unavoidable. This conception is closer to the Jewish idea because the inevitability of progress implies the intervention of God and movement toward a Messianic era. In several Christian versions of this theory—like those of Augustine, Fichte, and Hegel—the emphasis is on God, who has preordained a providential plan, so that from the earthly city man eventually reaches the city of God. The dialogue between God and man becomes an almost divine monologue.

In the Jewish conception, the Messianic era will arrive right here on earth, rather than only in heaven; the dialogue between God and man is the interaction between God and history.

Having laid out some of the crucial implications of Abraham's revelation during that fateful dusk, we may now resume our discussion of him.

CHAPTER

II

Starting with the
Breaking of the Idols

Sacrifice of the Patriarch Abraham by Titian

I shall here take up the story of Abraham with an episode of fundamental importance in his life, as reported not in the Book of Genesis but in the Midrash.

Although not comparable in authority with the Old Testament, the Midrash has always been an important medium for the expression of Jewish thought. It was begun in the year 444 B.C., twelve years after the Jews returned from the Babylonian exile, when Ezra summoned a large number of scholars and assigned to them the arduous task of writing a commentary on the Pentateuch aimed at revealing fully its allusive content.

The story of Abraham in the Midrash starts with his relation with his father Terah, a manufacturer and seller of idols. Enraged by the fact that people are coming to buy idols and are offering sacrifices to them, young Abraham takes up a stick, uses it to smash the idols into pieces, and then places the stick in the hand of the largest idol. When his father returns and asks Abraham what he has done, Abraham pretends that the idols quarreled among themselves, and that the biggest of them broke all the others. He points to the stick still in the idol's hand. Terah protests, "These idols have no knowledge. You, my son Abram, dare to make fun of me."

Clearly, Abraham wants to make the point that if the idols do not have even the power to move, how can they be the object of worship? But Terah is not inclined to agree with Abraham or to let him go unpunished. In Terah's eyes, his son has committed a sacrilege, and Terah takes his son to King Nimrod for judgment and punishment. Nimrod proposes to Abraham that he worship the fire. In a challenging spirit Abraham replies, "Let us worship water, which extinguishes fire." The king then agrees to worship water, whereupon Abraham says, "Let us rather worship the clouds which bear the water." The king agrees to worship the clouds. Unrelenting Abraham says, "Let us rather worship the winds which disperse the clouds." The king agrees to worship the wind. Abraham says, "Let us rather worship human beings, who withstand the wind." King Nimrod then understands that Abraham is making sport of him. The king decides to worship fire after all and orders that the insolent Abraham be put into the fire; but God saves him.

This myth is interesting on many counts: in what it affirms and in what it denies. What it affirms is directly related to our discussion in the previous chapter: there is only one God, incorporeal, invisible, eternal—transcending any matter—and He cannot be replaced by any other god or by an idol.

Then compare King Nimrod with Abraham. Nimrod is accommodating; he is willing to worship water instead of fire, clouds instead of water, wind instead of clouds. He wants to worship something that he can see or something that he can feel physically, like the wind. Abraham tantalizes him, wishing to demonstrate that all the things Nimrod is willing to worship are inferior to man. Why, then, not worship man? Only God is superior to man, and only Him is Abraham willing to worship. But the invisible God remained invisible to Nimrod.

STARTING WITH THE BREAKING OF THE IDOLS

Terah, Abraham's father, remains an insignificant figure; he is the last person in the Bible and in the Midrash to precede Judaism. With the breaking of the idols, a new era starts. Abraham—not Terah—is the first Jew, and he is the founder of the modern world, a world that will painfully, throughout centuries and centuries, try to overcome primitive ways of feeling, thinking, acting, and all the various forms of idolatry that are connected with them. The myth of the breaking of the idols represents the beginning of a long struggle by Judaism against religious concretization and other primitive attitudes of the mind. One of the recurring themes of the Pentateuch is this fight against the concrete gods. The gods of the surrounding polytheistic people are stigmatized as being "wood and stone" or "silver and gold."

The vividness of sense impressions, the element of surprise, and the scarcity of logical elaboration in primitive life give it a picturesque and fervid atmosphere that is particularly conducive to the conception of innumerable deities. Primitive man feels that the god actually resides in the physical object, be it a tree, an animal, or a stone; but somehow he does not fully understand the divine mysterious essence in the object. Thus he makes an effort to visualize or conceive of the god in a physical form: he transforms the object of contemplation so that the tree, the animal, the stone is perceived as a god. Idolatry is a form of response when something is perceived as vague and abstract and therefore threatening. The abstract "something" has to be concretized, made part of the material aspect of life. The world then appears as full of numberless particular small gods.

In the long history of humanity, however, life changes. The decline of primitive attitudes gives rise to the gradual development of more elaborate ideas, of concepts; people then have a less intense response to perceptual vividness. Progressively the earlier profusion of gods gives way to a more select number of them. In paganism we see a single god becoming responsible for a variety of phenomena. And whereas in the transitional periods between idolatry and paganism, the deities are believed to reside within objects or to belong to the same natural world as man, with time there is a gradual separation of the deity from physical things. The gods are cast out from the everyday material world and may even be relegated to a distant Olympus. From there, however, they continue to regulate the things with which they had once been identified.

Thus, although paganism makes possible the elevation of the gods to a higher realm of their own, this separation of deity from object is only the beginning of an abstraction. The god is again given a physical appearance; he is anthropomorphized. Most of his attributes are human, although he may be endowed with such superhuman properties as magical power and immortality.

Though Abraham is living in a time of idolatry, his rejection includes the paganism that is to come along with the idolatry that is present. In smashing the idols he becomes not only the prototype but the archetype * of the subsequent Jewish attitude toward life. Abraham becomes Avraham Avinu, Abraham our father, a living force in ancient Judaism and later in modern life.

Jewish history reveals how loyally Abraham's descendants have adhered to the way first shown by him. They have not embraced other gods. Indeed, they have at times suffered martyrdom rather than accept another faith. Their stiff necks have not bent either to worship emperors

* The word "archetype" is not used here in a Jungian sense.

or empresses transformed into gods. Shadrach, Mishach, and Abednego prefer to risk death rather than bow down to worship the gold image built by King Nebuchadnezzar. Akiva (50–135 C.E.), with his acceptance of death rather than submission to Roman paganism, is the shining example of a multitude of other Jews who followed.

True, the Jews often transgress, as witness the episode of the golden calf, narrated in Exodus. And throughout the course of Jewish history many have found that adherence to Abraham's ways was too difficult, and they have left the people of Israel—so great has the temptation always been to succumb to idolatries, whether literally by worshiping a visible deity, or by the worship of material goods, or by craving the advantages of belonging to a powerful majority, or by the neglect of "invisible values." But those who remained in the fold of Abraham have as a whole stuck to his principles throughout the millennia. For, clinging to "invisible" values, they have been forced to pay highly visible prices: the loss of human rights, the contempt and hatred of the masses, servitude, martyrdom, and death.

Abraham can be seen in a double role. On the one side, he is the prophet who declares the Imageless Transcendence; on the other side, he is the iconoclast, the one who destroys the idols who are gods to other people. With his teaching, could he have easily convinced people to barter the visible for the invisible, and to trade the traditions and the beliefs to which they had adhered since primordial times for something totally abstract? Could the Jewish people, living among other nations and other peoples, be easily understood? The answer is no. Even when other people embrace at least partially the Jewish principle of the Imageless Transcendence, they continue to see the Jew as an iconoclast, as the one who has destroyed their most cherished beliefs. The Jew not only challenges their ideas, but he places in doubt what for them has counted most. To this centuries-long conception of the Jew, mythical layers are added: thus the Jew who breaks idols, the descendant of Abraham, becomes the person who breaks all the gods, who eventually even kills god.

The Jew, who is one day to be accused of deicide, is the descendant of Abraham, who kills Nimrod's god. He is the bearer of the torch lighted by Abraham. To this day he is not seen as the advocate of the Imageless Transcendence. It is forgotten that Abraham's torch is that which illuminates one's steps to "walk in all His [God's] ways, to love Him, to serve the Lord your God with all your heart and with all your soul." * It is forgotten that it is the torch that shows how "to love and clothe the orphan, the widow, and the stranger which is among you," † which indicates that "If your enemy is hungry, give him bread to eat; and if he is thirsty, give him water to drink." ‡ It is forgotten that it is the torch that enlightens mankind "to love your neighbor as yourself." § This torch is viewed as the instrument of him who burns icons and kills other people's God.

THE ACCUSATION OF DEICIDE

The accusation of deicide has stood for untold generations between the Jews and Christianity, visiting horror and tragedy upon them. Perhaps with the accession of John

* Deuteronomy 10:12.
† Deuteronomy 10:19, 20.
‡ Proverbs 25:21.
§ Leviticus 19:17.

XXIII to the papal throne, a new era in Christian-Jewish relations was inaugurated—an era of understanding and, it is to be hoped, of love. Pope John XXIII promulgated the doctrine of brotherhood of men of all faiths and an attitude toward the Jews in particular which stands in sharp contrast to the traditional official position of the Roman Catholic Church. Under his direction the Ecumenical Council of 15 October 1965 produced a declaration deploring anti-Semitism and declaring that the crucifixion of Jesus Christ "cannot be attributed to all Jews, without distinction, then alive, nor the Jews of today."

And yet for centuries masses of Jews were killed for no other reason than that they were thought to be related by blood to those who had condemned Jesus Christ. No matter in what period they lived, they were called Christ-killers and as a group were held responsible for deicide. Especially during the Easter season Jews were frequently the object of violence from enraged crowds whose hostility was excited by the re-enactment of the Passion of Jesus Christ.

Quite often these Jews would be accused of having kidnaped and killed a Christian child for ritual purposes. This accusation, repeated from century to century, was the provocation for many pogroms and led thousands of Jews to death. Perhaps the child who was the presumed victim was again a symbol of Jesus Christ; perhaps in the myth there was a distant echo of the myth of Abraham, who is willing to sacrifice his son Isaac (see chapter 4). There is nothing in the holy books of Judaism, nor in the mores of the Jewish people, to justify the sacrifice of children to deities. Throughout the Pentateuch, and at least three times by the prophet Ezekiel, the practice is condemned.

But when a human being is hungry for violence, robbery, and murder—a hunger resulting from political frustration or oppression—an ancient myth can give the incensed masses the needed permission, the signal, to unchain their primitive instinct of aggression. The myth is often the myth of deicide. But the myth of deicide is itself a repetition of the myth created when Abraham "kills" Nimrod's god.

Pope John XXIII tried to put an end to this myth. His encyclical *Pacem in Terris* is the most advanced official Roman Catholic statement of religious freedom. For the first time in the history of the Church an encyclical was addressed not only to the Roman Catholic clergy and to Roman Catholics but to all people of good will, Christians and non-Christians. Forty-seven times it mentions the dignity of every human being, and several times refers to "the equality of the natural dignity of all men." Although John XXIII, who was seventy-seven when he was elected pope, had died when the declaration of the Second Ecumenical Council was issued, he must be considered its real author. For he had prepared the ground for the declaration in a series of actions in which he tried to set in motion a rapid change of attitude on the part of the Church toward the Jews. In March 1969, in the Church of Saint Mary in Jerusalem, and in Rome, the Good Friday prayer was read in his presence for the first time omitting the words *"perfidi Judaei"* ("perfidious Jews"). He requested that those lines of Matthew according to which the responsibility for the blood of Jesus may be accounted to the Jews and their children, be omitted from any prayer. He also organized a secretariat to study the relations of Roman Catholics toward non-Christians and especially Jews.

The declaration of the Ecumenical Council says that the

crucifixion of Jesus Christ "cannot be attributed to all Jews, without distinction, then alive, nor to the Jews of today." This is the same as saying that no Greeks living today, nor all Greeks living in 399 B.C., are or were responsible for the trial and execution of Socrates, or that no Italians living today, nor all the Italians living in 1498, are or were responsible for the trial and execution of Girolamo Savonarola. All three of these statements are not only truths, but truisms, something that the man in the street can immediately understand. Pope John's greatness, then, does not consist of something new but of his taking the first necessary steps toward removing the power of a dangerous hurtful myth that has been kept alive for nearly two thousand years—a myth that itself grew out of another two-thousand-year-old myth based on Abraham's destruction of Nimrod's god.

What has kept the tradition of blaming the Jews so strong down through the centuries?

First, let us examine the facts as they are described in the Gospels, and especially in the Gospel of Matthew—in the opinion of many (though I disagree), the source of a great deal of anti-Semitism.

According to Matthew, the high priest Caiaphas, along with other elders alarmed by the revolutionary teachings of Jesus, had him arrested, falsely accused, and condemned to death. He was put to death by crucifixion, the barbaric method introduced by the Romans. According to Matthew, people who approvingly witnessed the crucifixion said, "His blood be on us and on our children."

The crucifixion is indeed a horrible event: an innocent teacher of a new ethic is murdered in a most atrocious way because a few members of the established priesthood see in his teaching a threat to their power. History has repeatedly witnessed terrible injustices of this kind. Socrates was put to death because of his teaching. Some of the greatest men in human history, like Savonarola, Abraham Lincoln, Mahatma Gandhi, Martin Luther King, were murdered because of their life missions.

In the case of Jesus, as narrated in the Gospel, Caiaphas and the scribes must be considered among the most abominable human beings of their generation. The crowd, too, excited by the demagogues, deserves our utter contempt. However, the gathering who witnessed the crucifixion—two hundred people at most—cannot represent the whole Jewish people living then. They spoke only for themselves, and their actions must be accounted to them and to them only. When they say, "His blood be on us *and our children*," they speak without warrant. They certainly did not speak for all the Jews, who—with the exception of a few—had nothing to do with the crime. Moreover, why should these people be empowered to determine the fate of their children? Devout Christians, following Christ's teaching of love, mercy, and justice, can certainly not have interpreted Matthew's words as meaning that all Jews living at the time of Christ, not to speak of all the subsequent generations of Jews, were to be responsible for killing Jesus Christ. To do so would be, in the framework of Christian theology, to consider Jews as being not once but twice marked at birth: the first time by original sin because of what Adam did; the second time because of what Caiaphas and his followers did.

Why, then, was an effort made to interpret Matthew in this distorted way? Why were the Jews called Christ killers and accused of deicide? Why was no consideration given to the fact that the sentence about the responsibility for Jesus' blood is not found in the Gospels of Mark, Luke, and John? Obviously there were other forces operating which predisposed the Christians to such an interpretation.

What were these forces? The writings of Saul of Tarsus, later known as Paul, the founder of organized Christianity, give us a clue. Contrary to the Gospels, which may be read in the same mythical spirit as Genesis, Paul's letters are historical documents and must be evaluated as such. Except for the letter to the Hebrews, which, even in the ecclesiastic tradition, was not attributed to Paul at the beginning of the Christian era, there seems to be no doubt that the letters are Paul's authentic writings.

Paul gives a great deal of consideration to the Jews. At the same time that he wants to spread the new Christian faith to the Greeks and to the Romans, he also wants to convince the Jews to embrace it, and he fervently hopes that they will. In the letter to the Romans he states that God has not repudiated His people. Paul himself is an "Israelite, a descendant of Abraham, a member of the tribe of Benjamin." * Paul leaves the door open to the Jews. They may come and they will be accepted. There is no mention of the sin transmitted by Caiaphas. Israel, too, has heard the voice of Christ, but has not yet accepted it.† Although he hopes that the Jews will accept the new faith, he is aware of having much more success with the Gentiles. He writes that the error of the Jews may become the salvation of the Pagans because he will address his apostolic mission mainly to the Pagans; nevertheless, the Jews may also benefit. "I am an apostle to the Gentiles, I magnify my

* Romans 11:1.
† Romans 10:18, 19.

ministry in order to make my fellow Jews jealous, and thus save some of them." * Again, addressing himself to the Romans, he says,

> Lest you be wise in your own conceits, I want you to understand this mystery, brethren: a hardening has come upon part of Israel, until the full number of the Gentiles come in, and so all Israel will be saved; as it is written.
>
> > "The Deliverer will come from Zion
> > he will banish ungodliness from Jacob;
> > and this will be my covenant with them
> > when I take away their sins."
> >
> > [Isaiah 59:20–21]
>
> As regards the gospel they are enemies of God, for your sake; but as regards election they are beloved for the sake of their forefathers. For the gifts and the call of God are irrevocable.†

Paul is obviously displeased that the Jews do not accept the new faith, but he does not reject them. His letter to the Romans is a way to reach both Greeks and Jews—a difficult task—and to show them the advantage in accepting Christ in ways that appeal to both of them. Thus circumcision is not necessary because *Abraham was selected by God* before he was circumcised. Abraham has faith in God even when it is almost impossible to have faith, and he is rewarded even though he is not circumcised.‡ In this letter Paul is careful to keep his concern in this delicate balance between Jews and Greeks, but at this point he still seems to prefer the Jews. He writes, "For I am not ashamed of the gospel: it is the power of God for salvation to every one who has faith, to the Jew first and also to the Greek." §

* Romans 11:13.
† Romans 11:25–29.
‡ Romans 4:10–11.
§ Romans 1:16.

A small minority of Jews, but certainly more Jews than actually witnessed the crucifixion, have at this point embraced Christianity. About forty years have passed, and the promised Second Coming of the Messiah has not taken place. Swords have not been made into plowshares. The converted Jews are losing hope and faith and are contemplating returning to Judaism. Paul's letter is an attempt to restore their faith in Christianity.

In the writings of Paul, and to some extent in the other books of the New Testament, one can see an increasing impatience with the Jews because while they should be the first to embrace Christianity, they are proving the most reluctant to accept it. Paul's anger toward the Jews reaches its acme in the first letter to the Christians of Thessalonica, in which he speaks of the Jews only tangentially, but says enough to show what he now thinks of them.

> For you [Thessalonians] suffered the same things from your own countrymen as they did from the Jews, who killed both the Lord Jesus and the prophets, and drove us out and displeased God and oppose all men by hindering us from speaking to the Gentiles that they may be saved—so as always to fill up the measure of their sins. But God's wrath has come upon them at last.*

Here, for the first time, Paul speaks of the Jews as the killers of Jesus. He attributes the Jewish opposition to the dissemination of Christianity among Gentiles to the Jews' desire that the souls of these Gentiles should not be saved. In this way the Jews "fill up the measure of their sins." "But God's wrath [referring to the defeat of the Jews at the hands of the Romans] has come upon them at last." It seems almost incredible that the man who composed the most

* 1 Thessalonians 2:14, 15.

beautiful hymn to love ever written in his letter to the Corinthians * could now express so much hatred. Together with the misinterpreted passages of Matthew, these words have directly or indirectly caused massacres of Jews throughout the centuries. Could Paul imagine that his words would help to nourish for centuries the climate of hatred that eventually made it possible, during the Second World War, for forty-three thousand Thessalonian Jews (far more people than the total number of the early Thessalonian Christians) to undergo—at the hands of German Christians, duly baptized in the name of Christ—mass robbery, forced labor, slavery, atrocious torture, and finally extermination?

Other Christian writings have had the same virulent effect. One more example will suffice—a passage from William L. Shirer's *The Rise and Fall of the Third Reich.*

> It is difficult to understand the behavior of most German Protestants in the first Nazi years unless one is aware of two things: their history and the influence of Martin Luther. The great founder of Protestantism was both a passionate anti-Semite and a ferocious believer in absolute obedience to political authority. He wanted Germany rid of the Jews and when they were sent away he advised that they be deprived of "all their cash and jewels and silver and gold" and, furthermore, "that their synagogues or schools be set on fire, that their houses be broken up and destroyed . . . and they be put under a roof or stable, like the gypsies . . . in misery and captivity as they incessantly lament and complain to God about us"—advice that was literally followed four centuries later by Hitler, Goering, and Himmler.†

* Corinthians 13:1–13.

† William L. Shirer, *The Rise and Fall of the Third Reich: A History of Nazi Germany* (New York: Simon & Schuster, 1960), p. 236. In a courageous spirit Shirer footnoted the passage as follows: "To avoid misunderstanding, it might be well to point out here that the author [William L. Shirer] is a Protestant."

Issues of religious ethics are not what Paul is arguing about with the Jews. In one of the final passages of the important letter to the Galatians he quotes a passage of the Old Testament * and writes, "For the whole law is fulfilled in one word: you shall love your neighbor as yourself." † His quarrel with the Jews is only their refusal to accept Christianity, which necessitates the acceptance of the divinity of Christ and the recognition of Jesus as the Messiah. In other words, Abraham's descendants are doing it again: denying the divinity of another god. They "kill" the Christian god not so much through crucifixion as, metaphorically—or if you will, spiritually—by not accepting the divinity of Christ. Their adherence to the Torah (Paul says he has come to fulfill it by abrogating it) proves to be for them stronger than the apostle's word. It is this about the Jews that disturbs Paul, and that has disturbed generations of Christian leaders in all the subsequent centuries.

Could the Jews have accepted the divinity of Christ? The answer is no. They would have accepted that he was created in the image of God. They would have accepted that in him, as in every human being, there was a divine spirit, a divine spark. If a climate of understanding and reciprocal acceptance had been possible among Christians and Jews, Jews would probably to a considerable extent have accepted the moral teachings of Jesus, recognized him as a teacher of ethics, as a master or a prophet, who offered the possibility of a different understanding of the Pentateuch and of the Prophets. However, they could not accept such basic tenets of Christianity as the Resurrection, Christ's divinity, Christ as the son of God (unless, as

* Leviticus 19:18.
† Galatians 5:14.

has been said, this expression is taken to mean that every human being is a child of God). To accept these tenets would mean giving up Abraham's principles and mission.

Thus the Jew again becomes a deicide. Abraham's legacy is sustained at untold cost because Christianity is eventually victorious in the pagan world, in Greece and Rome. Paul is right in the end to have concentrated on proselytizing the Greeks and the Romans rather than the Jews. The ideas that the Jews rejected were more easily understood by the pagans who conceived of their gods in human forms and not as Imageless Transcendence. Indeed, Christianity in general has not been so reluctant to attribute to special human beings certain characteristics that for Judaism belong exclusively to God. As late as 18 July 1870, the Ecumenical Council in Rome affirmed the dogma of papal infallibility. When this new dogma came to a vote, five hundred fifty-three bishops voted in favor, and only two against. In the Pentateuch, on the other hand, it is reported that Moses, too, is capable of error. In the Haggadah, the account of the liberation of their forefathers from Egyptian slavery read by Jews during the Passover Seder, not even *once* is the name of the leader of the Jews, Moses, mentioned: the Jews are afraid of arousing any tendencies to deify Moses.

In any case, it would take entire libraries to describe the persecutions endured by the Jews in Christian countries, from the massacres during the Crusades to their extermination in twentieth-century Germany. The acts of the ecumenical councils and the papal bulls provide vivid examples. Since the first ecumenical council, which took place in Nicea in the year 325 C.E., bishops would periodically get together for the purpose of elaborating and clarifying matters pertaining to the Christian religion and relations with other people. To take one example: in the fourth Lateran council, which took place in the year 1215, it was stated that the usury of the Jews would, in a brief time, exhaust the wealth of the Christians. Jews, too, must pay taxes to the churches. They must dress so as to be immediately recognizable as Jews. During Easter week they must "not dare to appear in public" places. Since they have blasphemed Christ (by not recognizing him as God), they should be forbidden from holding public offices. Jews who had converted to Christianity should not be permitted to return to Judaism because "it is less bad not to know the way of the Lord, than to abandon such a way after having known it." Moreover, crusaders should not be required to pay interest for money borrowed from Jews.

In the Council of Basel, Ferrara, Florence, and Rome, which took place over the course of various sessions between the years 1431 and 1445, it was reaffirmed that Jews and other heretics could not acquire eternal life but would go into the eternal fire prepared for the devil.

In 1555, Pope Paul IV issued an infamous bull known as *Cum Nimis Absurdum*. Beginning with these Latin words, it declared that it was absurd that Jews, guilty of the world's greatest crime (the killing of Jesus), should be allowed freedom or receive Christian compassion. Jews must live apart from the Christian population, have only one synagogue, wear a yellow badge. They were forbidden to employ Christian servants, to work on Christian holidays, to lend money to Christians, or even to speak to Christians. They were allowed to sell only second-hand merchandise, or suits or dresses rejected by all other merchants. Jewish doctors were forbidden to treat Christian patients, could not be called "mister," and had all official privileges canceled. Only after 1938 was Hitler himself to go further than these restrictions.

The words of Paul—"Love bears all things, hopes all things, believes all things, endures all things"—have a sublime ring, but one could also say that *hate,* based on two-thousand-year-old religious prejudice and bigotry, *bears* all its terrible atrocities to the victims, *hopes* the worst for the victim, *believes* that they are criminals to be killed on earth and condemned to eternal fire, and *endures* all atrocities done to them, including starvation, hanging, gas chambers, tying together the legs of women in labor, and making lampshades out of human skin. We have to ask how people who had long professed to believe in the teachings of Jesus and Paul could come in the end to perpetrate these horrors. I do not even faintly suggest that these horrors were in any way connected to the intentions of Jesus or Paul. Nevertheless, it must be admitted that, being human, the Christian leaders erred in believing that their teachings would lead to universal brotherhood. How far is all of this misconception from the idea that because of Abraham *all* nations and *all* families of the earth would be blessed! *

It is to be hoped that all this hatred belongs to the past. Christian leaders seem no longer to be incensed over the fact that Jews do not believe in the divinity of Christ. They have certainly realized that the attitude of the Jews was not inspired by hate for Christianity or Christians. From Abraham to the present, Jews have rarely tried to impose their beliefs on others; and except for occasional, and brief periods, proselytism has been at a minimum. Even Abraham's main purpose is not to force Nimrod to convert. It has always been a practice of Judaism to respect the religious feelings and ideas of other people. The Jews have always known that they are a tiny minority, and that they will always be so. They preach not might or power but

* Genesis 12:3.

the spirit of God. In the words of Joel, they hope for the day when the spirit of the Lord will be on all flesh,* and, with Isaiah, for the time "when the earth shall be full of the knowledge of the Lord as the waters cover the sea." †

In adopting the name of John, Pope John Paul II has indicated his desire to continue on in the great humanitarian tradition of his predecessor John XXIII. Such an intention on the part of John Paul II could have an even greater impact on Christian attitudes toward Jews, for he comes from a land where anti-Semitism has raged for centuries.

Let me quote once more the important passage from Paul's letter to the Galatians: "For the whole law is fulfilled in one word, 'You shall love your neighbor as yourself.' But if you bite and devour one another, take heed that you are not consumed by one another." ‡ "Your neighbor" is a category that includes any inhabitant of the earth, neighbor to you insofar as he shares this planet with you. It is through this universal love, stemming from Abraham's benediction, that all families of the earth will be blessed.

THE SO-CALLED DEATH OF GOD

In the modern world, and especially at the present moment, Christianity and Judaism must together face the challenge of those who, following Nietzsche, have proclaimed that God is dead. They are the ones, and only they, who are the would-be deicides. All the descendants of Abraham together, those Jews descended from him by blood and spirit

* Joel 3:1–2.
† Isaiah 11:9.
‡ Galatians 5:14–15.

along with those who descend from him in spirit only, must oppose this challenge, which seems to have spread through vast segments of our society. These new would-be deicides cannot accept the Imageless Transcendence as conceived by Abraham. No matter whether by God one means a personal god, or an abstract spirit, or some level of the Absolute that transcends the relativity of the world—or even an ideal of the Absolute, or an ideal of justice, love, and mercy, or a concept or an experience of the divine— God has been declared dead on the ground that all visions or conceptions or beliefs about Him are meaningless. Those who declare Him so are blind to the invisible, deaf to the eternal voice. Indeed, they cannot kill Him, but they can deaden the feeling or idea of His existence in their hearts and minds.

Why have so many people become impervious, deaf, to the spiritual? Many things have contributed to their condition, but its fundamental result is that people become like King Nimrod: they see and acknowledge only what is visible. We are concerned with the question of values, and for many people values are not discernible properties. They are not discernible if we look at them with eyes trained to see different categories of things—eyes that may be effective and accurate in the world of fact. They may be eyes trained for good purposes, like the pursuit of scientific discovery, or for bad purposes, like the fashioning of idols. But whatever the eyes see is only secular and earthly.

It is beyond the purpose of this book to study in detail all the conditions that have led to the desanctification of life in our contemporary society, but I shall discuss a few of them briefly. Although I shall review them separately, the reader can easily realize that all of them are interrelated, and that each of them in some way implies all of them.

Overall Embracing Determinism

As I have discussed before, particularly in my book *The Will to Be Human*,* determinism as a way of explaining the universe has become widely accepted in all areas of human understanding. Determinism affirms that every effect or event has an ineluctable or necessary cause to be found in the physical world. However, even in relation to the physical cosmos the principle of uncertainty or indeterminacy formulated by Heisenberg has led many to doubt that strict determinism can be applied to individual subatomic occurrences (the world of electrons).

But even if a deterministic causality reigns supreme in the physical world, until recently the human being was considered to have overcome this determinism by virtue of his free will. A human being can choose; he is not ineluctably chained to previous causes. On the other hand, certain modern sciences have tried to demonstrate that such things as genetic conditions, endocrinological functions, sociological factors, family influences, and so forth, determine our feelings, thoughts, and actions. The functions of ours that we consider free are, in the view of these sciences, the *ineluctable* sequence of things that have occurred before. They would not escape determinism. Even psychoanalysis has shown that many of our actions and thoughts are not free as they seem to be, but the result of unconscious psychological mechanisms of which we do not even know the existence. All this is to a large extent true. The crux of the matter, however, hinges on the word "ineluctable." One cannot maintain that human actions are completely free; but on the other hand, it is equally excessive to insist that we are completely unfree, completely

* New York: Quadrangle, 1972.

conditioned by inner and external circumstances. If we were so conditioned, we would be condemned to a slavery far worse than the kind imposed by the harshest tyrant or dictator.

I believe that Freud has also been difficult to understand on the subject of personal freedom, to some extent because of his own ambivalence or lack of clarity about it. In spite of observations that led him in the opposite direction, he wanted very much to be able to adopt the positivistic ideas of the nineteenth century. He said that to a large extent we do not live but *are lived*—that is, we are compelled to live in accordance with the dictates of our unconscious motivation, stemming from the id. But he also said that the main aim of psychoanalysis is to remove the restrictions imposed by repressive forces on the free will, so that the human being can become free and capable of choosing. "Where id was, ego shall be." The id is not free, but the ego is, at least to some extent. Thus, in spite of certain ambiguous statements of Freud's, psychoanalysis has assumed a major role in the field of ethics. It is actually the main psychological science that reaffirms the prerogative of man to have some degree of free will. It is the science that aims precisely at enlarging man's margin of free will. Other psychological schools, and especially behaviorism, categorically deny the human being any possibility of will. Burrhus Frederick Skinner, the best-known living behaviorist, has repeatedly stated that will plays no role in our life. In his book *Beyond Freedom and Dignity*,* he writes that there is no such thing as autonomous man. Man does not act; he responds. Hidden emotions, purposes, deliberations, values, personalities, character, unconscious aspira-

---

* New York: Alfred A. Knopf, 1971.

tions, goals, images, and imaginations are fictitious concepts. Of course, these concepts and feelings *are invisible* and are the foundations of *invisible values.* According to Skinner, the only way man can better himself is by devising more adequate methods of control. Skinner thus advocates that we give up our illusion of freedom and get busy learning how to control our lives by eliciting the conditioned reflexes that best fit our needs.

In *The Will to Be Human,* I agree that man is not *totally* autonomous, but I show that it is possible for him to increase his margin of autonomy. He may also choose to become more and more conditioned and less and less capable of choosing. In my book I describe the origin of the will in the human being, the various psychological steps by which this function comes to exist, its vicissitudes and abnormal alterations. In my opinion, will as the capacity to make and implement choices is the culmination and integration of all other psychologic functions; it represents more than anything else the humanity of the species Homo sapiens in its holistic aspect.

The cultural or social forces that today portray man as totally conditioned, programmed, and without any role in determining his own life deny dualism and interactionism and remove from the image of man one of those five characteristics that permit us to see him as having been created in the image of God. It is thus an easy step from determinism to the denial of God. Kahler correctly states that "the mere process of thinking implies that we are seeking what is right and true and rejecting what is wrong." * *"Cogito ergo sum"* implies *"Cogito ergo volo"*: "I think, therefore I will."

* Erich Kahler, *The Tower and the Abyss* (New York: Braziller, 1957).

Abraham and the Contemporary Mind

Decline of the Historical

When we stress determinism, which rules the physical cosmos,* we focus on the cosmic and we minimize the historical. The historical dimension enters the picture with the appearance of man on this planet. It adds the element of free will because history is the result of the will of a few individual men or of the will of collectivities acting under the influence of sociopolitical-economic forces. Some social forces affect human beings in ways that remain unconscious, but some do not. Even Emile Durkheim, the French sociologist, in referring to the influence of society on the individual, speaks of collective consciousness.

The decline of the historical sense encompasses many areas. It may include whatever has been made by man—that is, human culture—or it may simply be a lack of interest in the study of history.

In the 1960s there was a period of radical revision when the value of what had always been considered the best in Western culture—like the works of Homer, Plato, Sophocles, Dante, Shakespeare—was called into question. The vociferous and rather conspicuous minority responsible for this revision of attitudes did not go as far as the Nazis did and burn the books on their index, but they did popularize a philistine contempt for the cultural heritage; this contempt has not yet been completely wiped out. Those who contested the value of the culture expressed the idea that classical works were *not relevant* to man's daily existence. They

* According to Capek, determinism rules only the mesocosmos in which we live, a world that could be interpreted according to the Euclidian-Newtonian-Kantian perspective. It does not rule the microcosm (a world of subatomic dimensions) or the macrocosm (a world larger than solar systems) in which the Einsteinian-Heisenbergian physics applies. M. Capek, *The Philosophical Impact of Contemporary Physics* (New York: Nostrand, 1964).

76

obviously confused what is not *immediately relevant* with what is *irrelevant*. The study of Plato and Shakespeare may not be relevant to the question of what one should choose to eat for breakfast or what kind of cigarette one should smoke, but the reading of these authors cannot leave unaffected people who understand them. The effect may not be immediate or readily apparent, but generally it remains in the inner life of the individual for a lifetime.

Such philistine excesses have now subsided, but they have left an indelible imprint. Departments of philosophy, classics, and history have decreased in number in American colleges. The young are less interested in these fields and are discouraged by their families and advisers from pursuing them. The prominent historian, J. H. Plumb, has been moved to write a book called *The Death of the Past*.* How can a historian posit a question like the death of the past? Is the so-called death of the past connected with the so-called death of God?

Indeed, the study of history may seem difficult to defend. Has the study of history in the past or in recent times led to a better understanding of humanity? Has it modified human life in such a way as to prevent evil? What good has studying history done when in our own time we have had a Hitler, a Stalin, a Hiroshima? The old Latin saying *"Historia magistra vitae"* ("History, teacher of life") seems not to have proved valid. Although man has made some progress since the time when he was a cannibal, the progress has been too little and too slow. And yet such great thinkers as Thucydides, Tacitus, and Machiavelli, and in our time the German philosopher Karl Jaspers, have insisted that history has much to teach, that the study

* J. H. Plumb, *The Death of the Past* (Boston: Houghton Mifflin, 1970).

of the past is indeed important and relevant to the issues confronted by any generation of men. Upholding the belief that we are not able to learn from the past is tantamount to advocating a return to an animal-like state where —like horses, dogs, and cows, who cannot transmit what they have learned—each new generation is not transformed by a cultural heritage.

In truth, however, history has not always been taught in a pertinent, accurate, and unbiased way. Often historians and teachers of history have transmitted a particular cultural slant of which they themselves were not aware. In many countries (but especially in England, Germany, and Italy) an elite group of thinkers has apotheosized the national character and national destiny and has rewritten history accordingly. In other cases history has been edited to minimize or soft-pedal all the atrocities—the persecutions, the massacres, the enslavements—that litter the human landscape. Perhaps historians, and especially teachers of history, have not revealed the full extent of these barbaric acts in order to protect either some specific groups of men or mankind as a whole. Teachers have unconsciously, or half-consciously, succumbed to social and psychological pressure to ignore or psychologically to deny events that incriminate basic institutions. They justify such omissions on the grounds of "protecting the young readers from psychological trauma" or defend them because the material is deemed not central to the main historical context. But what could be more important than the study of atrocities if one's purpose is to prevent their repetition?

Something else that has indeed made history seem less relevant is its presentation as *a mere sequence of facts*— political, economic, social, geographic, and so forth—unconnected values. Some people advocate that the study of history should be undertaken only in accordance with a scientific methodology, and that history should not be regarded as a process to be approached or evaluated from a moral point of view. But how is it possible to study the deeds of Nero, Hitler, or Stalin without passing moral judgment on them? In these cases, a detached attitude is artificial and harmful. The study of history will once more be valuable precisely when considerations of value are attached to it. But to stress values today, of course, means to face the opposition of those forces that wish to devalue values and of those who want to present history as devoid of the influences of morality and God. Studying history detached from values means to deny the wonderful aspect of interactionism between history and God which I discussed at the end of chapter 1. God has been ignored in history, but He has always been there. To modify Santayana's statement, had man been aware of His presence, man would not have been condemned to repeat history over and over again with all its errors and terrors.

The Focus on Science

Another characteristic associated with determinism is science, which in our time has reached undreamed-of dimensions. This is not the place to summarize the history of science or the enormous benefits bestowed by science on human beings. It need only be said that science has, among other things conquered terrible diseases, increased the quantity of food, facilitated communication, magnified human productivity, removed many dangers, and opened many geographical horizons, along with horizons of knowledge, previously closed to the masses. Science has an additional inherent value; it has done more to unify mankind than any ideology, law, or power. Science discovers laws that are as valid for the aborigine in Australia as for the professor at Harvard.

But scientific knowledge and control of nature which are not attached to values do not necessarily lead to good results. Science may lead to the construction of gas chambers as well as to the conquest of polio, to the dropping of a bomb on Hiroshima as well as to landing a man on the moon.

Many people see in the present crisis a realization of what the famous German sociologist Max Weber foresaw: the difficulty of maintaining an alliance between science and value leading to *"die Entzauberung der Welt"* ("the disenchantment of the world"). Those involved in this realization see science as completely indifferent to the meanings and values about which man cares. Even social science, which deals with human societies, most often is concerned with objective facts, not with subjective values. Science is concerned with the truth, not with the holy, the good, the beautiful. Whereas values vary from one society to another and from one individual to the next, facts as such have ultimately to be accepted by everybody.

When science contributes to evil, the fault is not with science itself but with the way science is used. Man cannot follow science with scientific methods only; for every act, even in science, insofar as it is human cannot be disconnected from values. The attempt at disconnection sooner or later leads science into the service of bad values, and the supposed beneficial actions of science may be diverted to sponsor the forces of evil.

Insofar as our industrial society is largely influenced or, more correctly, is molded by a science that tends to be deprived of values, this condition may lead to a complete removal of the spiritual from life. For the individual, as well as for the society, a *total* commitment to a scientific worldview may create a special and undesirable mentality. The individual may come to appreciate only efficiency and to disregard all other values, including the subjective and private aspects of himself.

The scientific methods of analyzing, quantifying, and translating into statistical data are useful when they are applied to scientific areas. When they are applied to the whole life of the individual, however, individualism is lost and depersonalization occurs. The qualities of life that are not reducible to the rigor or the exactitude of science are allowed to wither.

In academic training, science leads to such depersonalizing extremes only if separated by other cultural forces and only if science appropriates to itself the roles that belong to other fields. The progress of science must indeed be recognized as progress; but it should not be accompanied by a regress of the humanities. For several decades in many American colleges, education has been disproportionately scientific, and it is no wonder that many students have tended to become technicians or technocrats, or enamored only with the products of technique. The more scientifically oriented the education, the greater is the need for reaffirming the ethical and aesthetic values of the individual.

When one deals with the transcendental, positivistic and quantitative methodologies of science cannot be adopted. This limitation of science, of course, leads many scientists to deny the existence of anything that is transcendental. Among the scientists, there are, of course, exceptions, like Einstein. But they are, alas, not the rule.

Contrary to Weber and others, I do not think that science is the only culprit in this progressive devaluation of life. Periods of decadence held sway before the advent of modern science and before the Industrial Revolution. However, a science dissociated from values does predispose people to focus exclusively on what is immanent, and delays or actually makes impossible the ascent from immanence to transcendence. An example of how this science-without-values process works concerns the famous German pathologist Rudolph Virchow (1821–1902), whose ideas and work revolutionized medicine and to a large extent continue to influence medical science today. Virchow made many contributions to histology and pathology. When he retired from his position of director of the Institute of Pathology in Berlin, he left twenty-three thousand specimens that he had collected and studied.

This great scholar, utterly devoted to science, once said, "I have dissected many corpses in my life, but never yet come upon a soul." Of course he had trained himself to see only the visible. Although Virchow's remark may have been made facetiously, it actually reveals the philosophy that continues to influence medicine to this day. His principle that any disease is to be found in cellular pathology became one of the pillars on which the medical model is based. This formulation of the medical model does not seem appropriate to the field of psychiatry. If we were to adopt this model, we would have to assume that a disorder of the mind is like a disorder of the body, implying brain pathology or cellular pathology. This assumption would lead to two conclusions: (1) that psychiatric illnesses do not exist, are myths, or are just normal human conditions; or (2) that if a psychiatric condition is an illness, it cannot be functional but is necessarily based on cellular pathology. Both conclusions would be unacceptable to many modern psychiatrists, including myself. Many psychiatrists are instead willing to enlarge the medical model and accept the notions that the disabilities of the mental patients are real and pertain to medicine—both when they are, and when they are not, accompanied by cellular pathology.

Segmentation of Man

Another characteristic of modern times is to see man or his personality not as a unity but as a conglomeration of parts, functions, reflexes, or responses. David Hume, of course, denies the existence of a self. What he can see in himself are perceptions, impressions, and ideas, but not a permanent self. And behaviorists, too, say that a concept of self is not essential to the analysis of behavior: to them, we are only a collection of responses to our environment. Gilbert Ryle refers to the self as a ghost in the machine: for him, there is no permanent or enduring person; we react differently to different people; we are different in each category of situation.

And yet when I talk to the members of my family or to my friends or patients, I feel that I am the same Silvano Arieti. I recognize myself as a unity and a center of feeling, thinking, choosing, and acting even though external life confronts me with different situations. I also recognize certain enduring characteristics in myself. If I am cautious, I behave cautiously in driving a car, in dealing with people, in advancing hypotheses, in evaluating risks. If a friend of mine is impulsive, I recognize his impulsiveness in most, if not all, of his life experiences.

I see myself as more than a collection of interrelated functions and learned aptitudes. I am aware of my actions and responsible for them; I am to myself at least a unity, or a psychological totality. How can I espouse values if I am only an intermingling of functions? To which bundle of interconnections or sequences of reflexes will my actions be accounted? Obviously any scientific procedure requires the analysis of components, and therefore division and segmentation. But following that, a synthetic view or an experience or vision of unity has to be added, which should be better understood and appreciated after the analysis and the reintegration.

At the same time that man is attacked as a unity by these conceptions and deprived of his private inner self, he is also attacked from without. He belongs to a collectivity. He is induced to see himself less and less as an individual, and more and more as an easily interchangeable and expendable part of the collectivity. To be part of a collectivity means to learn to respond not to one's inner voices but to external stimuli. Being a collective man means conformity, anonymity, standardization, loss of uniqueness and autonomy. Of course, men and women must feel a part of their community, with a sense of nearness, of belonging, and of affectionate concern for that community. But such feelings are different from those of the collective man; his characteristics may lead directly or indirectly to alienation, violence, or materialism or to a combination of all three. *Alienation* is a word that means several different things. Marx used it in reference to the worker who, separated from the means of production which belong to the capitalist, becomes emotionally disconnected from his own work. In old-time psychiatry, alienation meant insanity. More recently in psychiatry and psychology, alienation has come to mean disconnection of a part of the self (or of the psyche) from its whole. The self does not feel or does not undergo experiences as it should. A part of the self is dissociated. In alienation, there is a mutilation of the soul (or of the psyche), and the individual has to live with his mutilated self.

Three types of such alienation have been described in recent psychological and psychiatric writings. In the first type the part of the self which is mutilated, or not experienced as fully alive, is the part that makes one relate to others. Thus the alienated person is the withdrawn individual, the introvert, the aloof or detached individual. A second type of alienation—described by psychoanalyst Karen Horney, in the early works of Erich Fromm, and by some novelists, like Camus in *The Stranger*—consists of disconnection from one's own feelings without being insane and without behaving in a way that is grossly abnormal.

In *The Will To Be Human*, I describe a third type of alienation where that part of the psyche which is in contact with the external environment is very efficient. Thus the individual does not seem alienated at all, but makes thousands of contacts, has many acquaintances, and is aware of myriad stimulations. He (or she) seems to experience all that the environment offers and to want to experience more. But the part which he does not experience (or which has undergone some mutilation) is his inner self, his inner life, the permanent self, the essence of his being. Instead of being in touch with this part of his psyche, the person affected by this form of alienation is in contact only with the external world. He neither acknowledges nor does he deny inner conflicts. He frowns upon inwardness, as if it were the enemy of relatedness, cooperation, human friendliness, solidarity, and feelings for others. The last thing he wants is to be called an introvert. He sees a journey homeward to his self as a form of detachment from the world and not as a source of life, inspiration, or as the entry into a universe of personal values and deep feelings. For him, extension replaces profundity. He would consider it strange to meditate on his inner problems or resources. The thing he has to do is to plunge himself into what is immediately offered—by the mass media, say, and by the interests, the fads, and the habits of others, especially of his peers. He must be constantly in contact, ready to react, to respond. He wants the environment to affect him but not to penetrate him; he wants to bathe in it. Rather than learning to create himself through the acquisition of concepts and values, he learns the superficial forms of behavior that permit him to deal with the habits of others and to adapt to the always changing environment. As time goes on he focuses more and more on the external world and becomes less aware of the inner self. If he ever feels an urge to recapture his inner self, the urge is promptly dismissed as foolish; for instance, he labels any sense of guilt "neurotic guilt."

The additional steps required for a person suffering this kind of alienation to proclaim the death of God are few indeed. He becomes deaf to inner voices, impervious to values, and concerned only with the visible. In many cases he becomes addicted to being a consumer, interested exclusively in material goods. Part of the external world, these goods replace inner values and become "idols of silver and stone." Of course, nowadays society abets a preoccupation with material goods. Whereas in former days the individual learned that to save and to be parsimonious was a virtue, he is now under constant pressure to "buy, buy, buy! consume, consume, consume!"

Another ill effect of the decline in the value of values is the great increase in crime throughout the world. People who are without intangible values and are chiefly interested in material goods are more inclined to commit crimes; in addition, society has become more tolerant of crime, less punitive toward the criminal, and has almost come to accept violence as a part of life. In some countries crime has become a daily occurrence as a political means for obtaining results. Holding hostages, kidnaping for ransom, committing robbery and murder on a grand scale—all have become almost ordinary deeds.

A person who commits an atrocious crime is often given a light sentence and paroled long before the expiration of his term. Whether this decrease in punishment is due to humanitarianism is debatable. Movie and television depictions of murderers in mystery and crime stories do not only tickle people as entertainment; often they glorify the criminal, especially if he is able to attain his end without getting caught. He becomes a special hero. Moreover, the fact that even some governments have been known to practice crime on a large scale provides additional justification for individual crime. Whether crime should always be forgiven in a spirit of mercy is a topic I shall return to in chapter 3. Certainly the people engaged in criminality want to believe that God is not watching or condemning them. Perhaps He is dead.

But those who are descendants of Abraham, either by blood and spirit or in spirit only, must reaffirm that Abraham's invisible God—God as a spiritual force and as a direction toward the highest values—is very much alive.

A Further Word on the Role of Science

A new science has recently been developed: futurology, or the study of what kind of future is in store for mankind. The predictions made by most futurologists seem to me pessimistic. They foresee not only what has been called the death of God, but also a total segmentation of man, or a total conditioning of every aspect of life. The human being would lose his individuality, would become more depersonalized, more limited in his capacity to choose, and more inclined to follow in a mechanical way the directions given to him by his group. With an increase in population, the scarcity of food, space, material goods, and even of oxygen, a rigid adherence to what the collective will requires, and a lessening call from one's inner self or from whatever autonomy has remained in one, will be the norm.

I am among those who still believe in man's willingness and ability to stop this disastrous course. I cannot even contemplate a state of affairs that, under the mask of appropriate and necessary control, would be a state of spiritual entropy. If humanity were to return to an appreciation of the precepts and values implied in Abraham's teachings and deeds, this apocalyptic end would be averted.

THE GREATEST VALUE

Innumerable are the values man recognizes; few are those he can espouse. The essence of a person consists largely of the values he espouses and to a lesser extent of the values he recognizes and respects. Truth, knowledge, justice, mercy, helpfulness are generally recognized values; as a rule they are appropriately and adequately discussed in writings devoted to ethics. You nourish your children not only with food but also with your affection, your advice, your concern, your teaching, your example. Their happiness is as important to you as your own; the unfolding of their life as important as yours. And they will see you their parents not just as the people who satisfy their physical needs but as those for whom they experience strong, affective attachment and love. You are the persons who have presented to your children the promise of life, a faith in tomorrow, a path to the richness of the universe. You are the adults who have made your own hopes the children's hopes in the atmosphere of family love.

Similarly, one can recognize in romantic love the dualistic essence of the human being. This love, of course, contains a sexual need. Nature or God has provided the beauty of the sexual experience to guarantee the perpetuation of the species. But poor is the love that remains the satisfaction of a sexual need and from which a spiritual need does not emerge. Your love partner is not only someone with whom you go to bed, although this is important and should not be minimized. If love is present, he or she is the person with whom you wish to share your basic attitudes toward life, your most essential values, your feeling for nature or art, the person in whose company you want to go to your synagogue or church, and the one with whom you share your great concern for the children you have had together. To be possessed by love is not something negative or something that detracts from the other activities of life. Love must possess you if it is to remain an inspirational force.

Let us select for further consideration the value called love, a value that almost every human being espouses. Unhappy and miserable indeed are those who do not espouse it.* All the spiritual descendants of Abraham espouse love

---

* For this section on love I draw liberally from the book I have written in collaboration with my son James, *Love Can Be Found* (New York: Harcourt, Brace, Jovanovich, 1977).

as the greatest value. Love is praised to the utmost degree in the Old Testament: love of God—"to walk in all His ways, to love Him, to serve the Lord your God with all your heart and all your soul"; * and love for human beings —"Love thy neighbor as thyself." †

At this point we shall consider, without being exhaustive, certain fundamental types of love. Two types that almost everyone acknowledges to be extremely powerful are family love and romantic love.

Family love (especially the love between parents and their children) begins in need. Parents respond to their offsprings' need for care, and the young of the human race, unlike the young of other species, require care for a long time. But this need, so far as it remains a biological need, does not yet involve love. Again the dualistic nature of the human being enters the picture. From the need of the body soon emerges a need of the spirit.

Real romantic love is a continuous exploration in both the physical and the spiritual parts of our essence. Unhappy is the state of affairs when the spiritual part does not emerge or grow, when the basic philosophies of life or religious attitudes diverge, or when after a period of infatuation the feeling becomes pallid and flaccid or turns into a trivialized set of habits.

Romantic love is seen by such thinkers as Denis De Rougemont ‡ as containing something negative in its essence—a contrast, an opposition, or a destructive element. The biblical view is more optimistic: witness the love between Isaac and Rebecca, Jacob and Rachel, Moses and Zipporah, Ruth and Boaz.

---

* Deuteronomy 10:19, 20.
† Leviticus 19:17.
‡ *Love in the Western World* (New York: Harper & Row, 1974).

From the two basic types of love—family love and romantic love—all other kinds of love derive. Other love may be less intense but, on the other hand, may embrace more in aim. Consider love for one's neighbor. Saint Paul elaborates on the sentence on love from Leviticus, "For the whole law is fulfilled in one word, 'Love thy neighbor as thyself.' " *

"Love thy neighbor as thyself." These biblical words seem first to indicate that a man should not love everyone, but should love only his neighbor, who is in close physical proximity and who shares common interests and desires.

Not everybody agrees even to this limited view of loving one's neighbor, however. Consistent with his aversion to biblical values, Nietzsche writes in *Thus Spake Zarathustra*, "Do I advise you to love the neighbor? I suggest rather to escape from the neighbor and to love those who are the farthest away from you. Higher than the love for the neighbor is the love for the man who is distant and has still to come." He was referring not to his fellow man but to his concept of the superman.

In any case, neighborly love is actually an extension of family love. The term *neighbor* is especially effective, for a neighbor is one we may see almost every day, someone on whom we are likely to call if we need help, whether the help be protection from a storm or fire or intruders or thieves.

In primitive societies the fact that people lived close together and traveled only short distances facilitated the bond of neighborly love. From ancient times people have varied as to the collectivity to be included in the circle of neighborly love. Anthropologists teach us that whereas members

---

* Galatians 5:14, 15.

of a primitive tribe might love one another, they sometimes even practiced cannibalism toward members of an enemy tribe. Fellow citizens or members of the same religion or ethnic group are often included in a circle of love, while all others are excluded. At times exclusion becomes a matter of policy, aimed at breeding solidarity within a group by distinguishing between "us" and "them." Only the great voices, like those of Isaiah and Jesus, rise to stir men toward a universal love for each other.

The message "Love thy neighbor as thyself" is not restricted to the neighbor in a literal sense but is aimed at including the whole of mankind. When we feel spiritually close to another person, he or she becomes a neighbor in our heart. Concerning the basic issues—birth, uncertainty, hope, growth, decay, death—we share the same destiny. The "neighbor" in this conception becomes a living entity in basic respects like you and yet other than you. You and the other become equal, as far as your love is concerned. Again the physical need for protection, for common defense, and for sharing of search for sustenance is transcended and becomes a spiritual bond.

Whereas you bestow family love on the members of your family, neighborly love must embrace the family of man. Every human being becomes a brother or a sister to you.

If you love a person whom you cannot judge on an individual basis as deserving or not deserving to be loved, your love acquires a special meaning. What is important in such love is not the special characteristics of the loved one, but *your loving attitude*, your willingness to include all the members of the collectivity. This type of love consists of a constellation of feelings and thoughts among which the following prevail: "My neighbor is my peer. I have respect and concern for him. I feel committed to the safeguard of his rights, uniqueness, and personal dignity. Although each one of us has his own individuality, we are all equal in the framework of these feelings and ideas. I expect my neighbor to feel for me as I feel for him. He is potentially my friend. That means that I am *potentially* ready to assume some responsibility for him." The concept of potentiality is important. Obviously we cannot be responsible for everything or for everybody. The potentiality becomes an actuality under special circumstances. Everyone then has access to our sense of responsibility, to our willingness to care and to help. Our participation will be dictated by our feelings, judgments, and commitments.

Does the biblical precept "Love thy neighbor as thyself" imply that you should love only your literal neighbor and those who in conceptual or affective ways you can consider your neighbor? Does it exclude loving yourself? Of course not. The Bible says, "Love thy neighbor *as* thyself." It does not say, "Love thy neighbor *instead of or more than* thyself." However, in some theological circles the saying has been interpreted, Love thy neighbor more than thyself. Do more for him than you do for yourself. As I understand the writings and teachings of Francis of Assisi, he believes that if you are a religious man and should find yourself in a lifeboat with another person, but with only enough water for one, you are expected to give the water to the other person. In the Jewish tradition, the situation is evaluated differently. If you are in some way responsible for the safety of the other person—if the other person is your child, or if you are a member of the crew and the other person is a passenger—you should certainly continue with your responsibilities and give the child or passenger water. But if you have no moral responsibility, you should consider that your blood is "just as red" as the other's, that your life is just as precious to God. You must love yourself at least as much as you love the other person. Some equitable solution will have to be reached. Fortunately, the circumstances under which one must save the other instead of oneself are extremely rare.

But can a person love himself as he loves others? Can he be both the lover and the beloved in a single reflexive relationship? Can he divide himself into subject and object?

Evidently the concept of self-love is not identical to that of love for others. The search for an understanding of self-love is not new. Aristotle calls self-love φιλautia, meaning the desire to appropriate to oneself the good and the beautiful.* Thomas Aquinas says that the individual loves himself when he loves his spiritual nature.†

To love oneself means first of all to accept oneself and therefore value the image that one has of himself. Accepting oneself does not mean one should consider oneself perfect. Self-love is also a striving to make oneself come closer to what one believes one ought to be. Recognizing one's limitations and shortcomings does not mean rejecting one's self, but it means that one attempts to overcome what can be overcome and to accept what cannot be changed. Loving oneself requires not that one be selfish, but rather that one engage oneself in one's own unfolding. Self-love is to be interpreted not in a monistic physical sense, as in the myth of Narcissus, but in a dualistic frame of reference with stress on the spiritual.

Having accepted the limitations of humanity, both religious and nonreligious, men retain an intense craving for what is not limited or relative. They seek what will sub-

---

* Aristotle, *Nichomachean Ethics* IX, 8, 1168a, 28.
† T. Aquinas 11. 11, 92b, a, h.

stitute clarity and certainty for mystery, perfection for imperfection, goodness for evil, justice for injustice, and love for hate. In other words, the religious person craves God, and the nonreligious one, who cannot conceive of a higher-than-human entity, craves a state of absolute perfection which, although alien to our human status, is not alien to our conceptions and feelings. The religious person calls his craving "love of God"; the nonreligious calls his "seeking the absolute."

In contrast with Leviticus, Aristotle believes, "It would be absurd for a man to love God." When the great philosopher made this declaration, he had in mind a god so far removed from human concerns that there was little one could love with one's heart—a god crucially different from Abraham's God. For Aristotle, God is a cause and effect which leads to the formation of the universe, somewhat similar to the primordial explosion which, according to some physicists, began the ever-outward expansion of the cosmos.

The position of Descartes is rather different. Toward the end of the Third Meditation, he writes:

> When I reflect on myself, I not only know that I am something incomplete, and dependent on another, which incessantly aspires after something which is better and greater than myself, but I also know that He on whom I depend possesses in Himself all the great things toward which I aspire (and the ideas of which I find within myself), and that not indefinitely or potentially alone, but really, actually, and infinitely, and that thus He is God.

Within this passage is a basic formula for loving God. If we believe that we are made in God's image, and yet recognize that we are unable to equal the model, we can then love that which we aspire to, namely, the fulfillment of our potentialities and the perfecting of our nature. Since we can always visualize a condition better than the one we are in—no matter how capable we are at something, we can always conceive of being better—we always have something to desire. This desire is mingled with a love for the desired state or object, and love becomes a continuous striving upward. Because man is finite and can never reach perfection, can never be like God, he will always be able to love God. Love for God thus becomes the greatest uplifting toward the transcendental.

A THEORY OF LOVE

Love can be interpreted in at least three different contexts: biologically, psychologically, and as a cosmic force. Although these three interpretations can be separated artificially for the sake of exposition, they are closely intertwined.

Biological Interpretation

Love is a complex of mechanisms and functions that assures the survival of the species. Sex leads to conception, pregnancy, and birth of offspring. Survival of the newborn is guaranteed by the love of adults, generally the parents. Thus, considered only from the biological point of view of the perpetuation of the species, love can be seen as an extension of the procreative value of sex. Moreover, romantic love renews or revamps sexual desire, making more probable new conceptions and new births. Although love exists among nonhuman animals also, with them it does not achieve the expansion nor does it undergo the transformations that take place in human beings. Human beings need a much larger amount of love than do other species due to particular circumstances: the longer period of dependency of the child relative to the young of other species; the marked physical vulnerability of the human being throughout life; the psychological insecurity caused by complicated interpersonal relations; the necessity for collective actions by human beings to secure nourishment, defense, and other essentials; the fairly constant sexual desire of men and women, which is not periodic as in nonhuman animals. Thus, for the human animal, biological evolution must provide not only sex, for the reproduction of the species, but also love, for its preservation. Every human being wishes to protect his love object, no matter whether he or she is a child, a parent, an erotic partner, or a friend. Conversely, we can say that love has favored evolution in certain directions by making survival easier for the loved person. The best way to nurture sex and love is to make them pleasant. Thus, though love is of great practical value in a biological or survival frame of reference, it also contains ingredients that cannot be viewed as purely physical.

What physiological mechanism makes possible the experience of love? What is the biological origin of its pleasantness? Since the time of the Greek physician Galen in the second century A.D. people have known that one experiences emotions not with one's heart, blood, bones, guts and glands, but literally with one's brain. Often people refer to emotions as residing in the heart, but the expression is now used metaphorically or as a residue from a conception that prevailed in ancient times when people believed that feelings were really mediated in one's anatomical heart. One loves with one's brain. Even today, this notion seems almost unbelievable to some people. What about sexual organs? For that part of love which consists of sexual functions, one certainly needs these organs. However, the pleasure that seems localized in the genital area or in other parts of the body is actually experienced in the brain. The central nervous system then projects the feeling peripherally (that is, psychologically externalizes it), and one believes that the sensation is occurring in several parts of the body, especially in the sexual organs.

Any pleasant sensation connected with sex or love is probably mediated in small areas of the limbic system of the brain, thought to be pleasure centers. But love is more than a pleasant sensation; it is a high-level emotion. Love must therefore involve those areas of the brain which the great American anatomist James Papez demonstrated as being responsible for emotional experience—areas that are part of what is now called "the Papez circle."

But human love has a great deal to do with ideas, expectations, evaluations, ideas, fantasies of all sorts—psychological phenomena that according to present knowledge, emerge in the parietal, occipital, temporal, and prefrontal lobes of the brain. Thus, love at a human level probably requires the involvement of the whole brain. But love is more than simply a function of a complicated network of neurons. It emerges as a psychological force which immediately acquires great meanings and values. The Cartesian dualism "brain-mind or psyche" asserts itself in the phenomenon of love, too.

Psychological Interpretation of Love

When love is seen as something that exists to a large extent for the sake of the lover, it is considered psychologically. The lover experiences the pleasantness of love and, as a consequence, alters his relatedness with the object of his love—a person, a thing, or an idea.

As a subjective phenomenon, love is one of the most intense forms of experience. Consciousness, which distinguishes human beings from the inanimate world, also puts the human in a state of separateness from other members of the species. Each person sees, hears, touches, thinks, smells, feels. Each tries to understand the surrounding world. Each person is a microcosm, but every person is within his or her own skin, separated from the rest of the world and therefore ultimately alone. One remains isolated unless one establishes bonds with others; and, indeed, people do establish such bonds with words, actions, thoughts, and feelings. But the particular form of intense consciousness that is love establishes the strongest possible bond between the individual and the objects of his or her love. The person who is in love does not feel alone. Even when absent, the beloved is in the company of the lover, thinks of the lover and/or longs for him or her.

The love received early in life from one's parents, is a gift generously given and liberally enjoyed; all the various other kinds of love are edifices that must be built throughout one's life with an inner law of harmony and proportion. Each human being is the architect of the edifice of his own love.

All kinds of love protect us from fear—fear of others, fear of some parts of oneself, fear of aloneness and loneliness. But except for the love of God, the various loves that the human being experiences do not bring about certainty; they bring an uncertain hope that transmutes itself not into anxiety but into a joyful expectation. Expectations of love are images enwrapped by love and thus are already partially satisfying, partially alleviating of desire, as if the expected reward were to some extent already present. Thus love permits dreams, reveries, and fantasies that become incentives to improve what one already has. The act of loving increases the value of the love object and at the same time makes the love grow.

Cosmic Interpretation of Love

We have so far considered love only as a human condition or function, or as having human significance. Can we envision human love in a cosmic context?

According to the majority of physicists, the second principle of thermodynamics indicates that the universe is proceeding toward a slow but inevitable death. Whoever or whatever has more energy than its surroundings is in the process of losing its energy. When a hot object is close to an object that has a lower temperature, the warmer object loses heat while the colder one acquires heat; eventually the two bodies will have the same temperature—that is, the same amount of thermal energy. The sun, provider of heat to the solar system, will also eventually be extinguished. Compounds of organic chemistry, like petroleum or blood, lose energy by being transformed into inorganic products. Whatever is alive, or has a complicated organic structure, will eventually decompose into inorganic substances and become dust. Mountains will eventually be lowered to sea level; the amoeba will end in decomposition just as a galaxy will. Whatever exists will sooner or later reach the state of simple atoms. Atoms of various elements may even break and return to the original state of the simplest element, the hydrogen atom. The return to the simplest form will constitute the death of the universe. This tendency toward decay, chaos, and dissolution is called *entropy*. Time moves only in one direction, toward increased entropy—continuously and ineluctably. People engaged in other areas of science have applied notions similar to that of entropy to their own fields. For instance, Freud formulated the concept of the death instinct; according to him, it exists in all of us as a counterpart of Eros, the life instinct, and is responsible for aggression.

Other people working in scientific fields believe that the picture is not so gloomy. If God created the world, or other natural forces gave origin to the universe, the event occurred through the origins of centers of concentrated energy, like suns. At least in our planet, life came into being—life consisting of complex molecules of organic compounds which have been built up from simple inorganic compounds. Although dissolution prevails and centers of energy and living entities constitute a minimal part of the universe, they do exist. In a universe characterized mainly by entropy, anti-entropic, or negative entropic, forces exist, too. In an adverse physical cosmos, life emerges, survives, and evolves heroically as an anti-entropic, constructive force. It partially transforms the chaotic complexity of the inorganic world into the organized complexity of the biological organism. With the advent of man, the organized complexity greatly expands. No matter what adverse judgment one can pass on mankind as a whole or on its parts, one recognizes in mankind a strong anti-entropic force, to be aligned with the forces that made the suns and the stars.

Man is seen again as created in the image of God, with five great faculties (described on page 23) which can now be considered in their anti-entropic aspect. In a cosmos that cannot be perfect because it is different from God, in a cosmos that decays, man becomes a force that tries and often succeeds in arresting or reversing this decay.

The first of man's five anti-entropic faculties is his reason, by which he observes, correlates, interprets, and tries to make sense of the apparent chaos. He permanently reorganizes the world with his observations, ideas, and deeds. The increasing entropy of the world is always confronted by a permanent reorganization and reconstruction accomplished by man's cognitive processes. Of course, the confrontation is unequal. Whatever man accomplishes is minimal in comparison to the decay of the cosmos, but the accomplishments are important to the planet earth.

If the human being were endowed only with reason, he would not be as constructive as he is. He could even use his reason for destructive purposes—and on many occasions he does bring destruction. In the totality of history, however, mankind has used reason predominantly for good purposes and has thus succeeded in surviving and following a direction toward progress. The human being has been able to choose a constructive course because he has also used his other anti-entropic qualities—the capacity to choose and a sense of oughtness, or an ethical sense. Rather than follow his impulsive desires, man predominantly chooses to do the good deed, to do what is ultimately good for mankind. In addition, man not only repeats and rebuilds what he already knows, but he continuously adds. By recombining what exists in different ways, he brings about new things in art, science, and literature. He creates. He becomes the partner of God in the act of creation. However vast is the realm of man's intellect, his capacity to choose, his ethical sense, and his urge to create, man would not actualize his anti-entropic capacities so successfully if he were not also moved by love. Virtue and knowledge, duty and creativity, are not enough.

Some people think that one need not differentiate love from virtue, and postulate a fifth anti-entropic faculty. Although a love is virtuous, it is in a special category of virtuous value. Whereas one may follow the dictates of virtue out of a sense of duty, one follows love because one *wishes* to do so. Love transcends its oughtness. Although one may choose to follow duties because one *wishes* to be duty-bound, the wish to love is predominantly in the love itself and not in its possible inherent oughtness. Of course there need be no contrast between the five anti-entropic faculties. Love is chosen and supported by reason and virtue and must contain elements of creativity.

Every type of love can become involved with an increasing number of feelings and ideas whose implications and ramifications intertwine more and more, giving rise to unsuspected new dimensions of feeling and understanding. Love can then become endless. To define love completely is impossible, just as it is impossible to define man completely in his psychological and spiritual essence.

The five characteristics of man discussed on page 23 and on page 102—and especially the capacity to love—indicate again that man stands at the point where nature and spirit meet and merge.

The definition of human love as a strong anti-entropic force sees man playing an active role in the outcome of cosmic affairs. This cosmic role for man has been one of the tenets of Judaism since Abraham, as will be further discussed in chapter 3.

Anti-entropic love is not only a dualistic concept but the

best form of interactionism. Love is the highest human feeling; it confronts God's cosmos with a spiritual embrace in accordance with His desire.

The events of the last few decades indicate that mankind should show reverence and love for the physical as well as for the human cosmos. Greed, the dominance of private interests, and hedonism, allied to the new industrial emphasis on consumption, have led to even greater injury to the environment. Some important raw materials approach exhaustion; the air, the sea, and the land tend to become polluted. It is my belief that this is only an interlude, however, and that it will soon be terminated by the overall anti-entropic drive of man.

The human psyche harbors a transcendental spirit and is thus as significant as the cosmos. As long as man is aware of his trancendental element, no metaphorical or actual deicide will occur. Like Abraham, man has the possibility, if he so chooses, to break the idols—be the idol a god of silver and stone, of greed, of power over others, of material goods, or, in the language of our day, of the pursuit of consumer goods.

CHAPTER

III

Sodom and Gomorrah

Detail of Abraham and Isaac by Donatello

MAN'S CONFRONTATION WITH GOD

We must return now to Genesis to consider the episode in the life of Abraham reported in chapter 18. God has made an important decision: He is going to punish two cities—Sodom and Gomorrah.

Sodom and Gomorrah are represented as evil incarnate. And as evil must be eliminated sooner or later, so must the two cities as well. But God does not wish to go ahead without first notifying Abraham, His partner and companion in the effort to purify mankind. The Lord says, "Shall I hide from Abraham what I am about to do, seeing that Abraham shall become a great and mighty nation, and in him all the nations of the earth shall be blessed?" God answers Himself, "No, for I have known him, to the end that he may command his children and his household after him that they may keep the way of the Lord, to do righteousness and justice." In other words, God wants to teach Abraham so that his descendants may do righteousness and justice. But the passage also seems to imply that God wants Abraham's consent before proceeding with His plan. A surprising situation! What does it mean? Why should the Omnipotent and Omniscient God need Abraham's consent? Of course, Abraham is a special person. God has previously told him,

Get thee out of thy country, and from thy kindred, and from thy father's house until the land that I will show thee. *And I will make of thee a great nation, and I will bless thee, and make thy name great, and be thus a blessing. And I will bless them that bless thee, and him that curseth thee will I curse. And in thee shall all the families of the earth be blessed.*

Thus Abraham is to be the founder of the nation that will receive the Divine Law, the Torah, the Bible; and—because of the Bible—not only the Jewish people but "all the families of the earth will be blessed."

So indeed Abraham is a special person. He has to leave his father's house, his own country, his own kindred in order to begin the history of the Jewish people. He has to wander among foreign people, and while he is to respect them as he respects his own, he is at the same time to retain his spiritual identity. Throughout his life he has no land he can call his own, but only *a promise* of a land. Almost every promise made to Abraham concerns not the present but the future. His life's history becomes a paradigm of the history of the Jewish people, and in a certain way of every individual Jew. Abraham is completely identified with the people who will descend from him. "I will make *thee* a great nation."

Nevertheless, although a special person, Abraham is a man. Why should God need his consent?

God treats Abraham as a partner, not as a passive follower. Even before God, human dignity receives the highest consideration. Moreover, the point of view of the man chosen to teach righteousness and justice to all the subsequent generations has to be respected in a special way and approached with a direct dialogue. How man must play an active role in the outcome of cosmic events was discussed in chapter 2. Here, a particular man, in order to be an example for future generations, is called upon to play a role in determining justice in connection with particular events. God's revelation to man is the Torah; but as the Talmud indicates, man's revelation to God (Abodah) and man's revelation to his fellow man (Gemilut Hassadim) are also crucial. Man must understand what is true and right, and he must be able to choose to practice compassion and love.

Dialogues between God and man, like the dialogue between God and Abraham, continue throughout the Old Testament in a historical framework. In this case the historical reality of Sodom and Gomorrah is the focus. Whereas in other faiths the salvation of the soul is all that counts, in the Old Testament this world counts very much too. Again, an absolute division between the transcendental and the immanent, between Heaven and earth, would be an extreme form of dualism. Rather, what is needed is interactionism. Whatever we consider spiritual should embrace the earthly and bring it closer to our ideal. If salvation occurs, it must be within the framework of history. Indeed, this salvation within history is what is needed more than ever on our planet if we are to live in peace and harmony and to pursue our human ideals without reference to questions of power and of privileged personal or national interests. Of course I am not advocating a theocratic state or the abolition of the separation between organized religion (or church) and state. No need exists to accept such restrictive and reactionary notions. What I do advocate is that we consider any political act from the standpoint not merely of the political as such—that is, in terms of power, practicality, and expedience—but also of the act's ethical or moral dimensions. Any decision about a Sodom and a

Gomorrah must be made only from the point of view of God, or of whatever one regards as a paradigm of moral values, with the free assent of man. Decisions have been taken this way in history, but only on rare occasions. More often, moral values allegedly inspired by God have been professed hypocritically, as when nations have waged religious wars against the peoples of other faiths, purportedly to defend the "true" faith but in reality to preserve or to increase worldly power. In all decisions if God has to be considered, man has to be considered, too. This is the meaning of God's consulting Abraham about the fate of Sodom and Gomorrah.

In the whole episode concerning Sodom and Gomorrah, Abraham is portrayed in a highly favorable light and at first makes a much better impression than God Himself. Abraham replies to God,

> Wilt Thou indeed sweep away the righteous with the wicked? Suppose there are fifty righteous within the city; wilt Thou then destroy the place and not spare it for the fifty righteous who are in it? That be far from Thee, to do after this manner, to slay the righteous with the wicked, so that the righteous fare as the wicked! That be far from Thee! Shall not the Judge of all the earth do right?

God reassures Abraham.

> If I find at Sodom fifty righteous men in the city, I will spare the whole place for their sake.

But Abraham begins to bargain.

> Behold now, I have taken upon me to speak unto the Lord, who am but dust and ashes. Suppose five of the fifty are lacking? Will thou destroy the whole city for lack of five?

God promises Abraham that He will not destroy the city if He finds only forty-five righteous persons there. The bargaining continues. What if there are only forty, or twenty, or ten? God promises again that He will save the city for the sake of ten righteous men.

In this episode Abraham is elevated to the role of defender of people. God is the judge, and Abraham the defender. Abraham assumes a humble posture. "I am made of ashes and dust." He reminds God of the material part of himself, but what he says bespeaks the spiritual part of him that has emerged from those ashes and dust. Passionately and magnanimously he pleads for the sinners.

Why ten? Why is the number ten allowed to stand for the possible salvation of the many? Tradition has it that Abraham is thinking of the flood, when there are only eight righteous people: Noah, his wife, and their three sons with their wives. Elsewhere in the Midrash it says that Abraham believes that there are ten righteous people in Sodom: his nephew Lot, Lot's wife, his four daughters and four sons-in-law, but that he is mistaken in thinking all of them righteous.

The important thing is the way Abraham defends the sinners. Not only does he appeal to justice ("That be far from Thee . . . to slay the righteous with the wicked"), but he includes in his defense a new and important argument: the virtue of a few should compensate for or neutralize the guilt of the multitude and justify forgiveness for all. Abraham's protest is the opposite of the protest of another important figure who appears much later in the Bible: Jonah. Jonah is full of indignation, as God has made a liar of him. Following God's request, he has gone to announce to the people of Nineveh that the city will be destroyed. But the people listen to Jonah and repent, and

God changes His resolution. Jonah wants to be the representative of the law of God, of a supreme, inflexible, irrevocable, divine command; he does not want to be an agent of salvation. He is chained to a formal sense of duty, rather than moved by feelings of goodness and mercy. Abraham, however, *is* moved by goodness and mercy.

We must again stress an added and significant aspect of this episode: not only does God consider Abraham a partner, somebody with whom He wants to discuss the fate of Sodom and Gomorrah, but Abraham on his side, has the boldness or, if you will, temerity to speak and argue with God. Abraham's attitude shows not only his compassion and desire to help his fellow man but also his feeling of entitlement to argue with God. *Even the authority of God should not be unquestioningly accepted.* (As we shall see in chapter 4, this point seems to contradict another episode in the life of Abraham, but that episode constitutes the most unusual circumstance.) What this story reveals is that man participates in a dialogue with God and has the right to state his case, to express his view. Whereas other faiths preach utmost submission and unquestioning acceptance of the divinity, Abraham and his descendants claim the right to argue. There are numerous other examples of this claim in the Bible: in Exodus 32:32, Moses asks God to forgive the Jews or otherwise cancel him from His Book. As did King Saul, although not successfully. In other words, in spite of his limitations and even before God, the human being is not requested to surrender his right to be himself, but is encouraged to interpret according to his judgment and to evaluate in his own way. God has given this personal dignity to the individual by creating him according to His own image.

The implications of Abraham's story go beyond religious issues. If a person is entitled to maintain a questioning attitude toward God, *a fortiori* (even more so) he should be entitled to maintain such an attitude toward other human beings. The descendants of Abraham become a stiff-necked people, a people who do not bend in front of emperors, kings, or despots. The human dignity of the other is to always be respected. One must face the other, even a dictator, with open-mindedness, respect, and compassion but not in such a way as to leave the authority unchallenged. Pharaoh, Torquemada, the czars, Hitler, and Stalin obviously could not accept this challenging attitude. A ludicrous form of denying the right to question a leader was advocated by fascism. A slogan preached and proclaimed over and over again, all over Italy, was *"Il Duce ha sempre ragione"* ("The Duce is always right"). The "good" Italian was not to challenge Mussolini's authority, but automatically, unconditionally, and with his whole devotion he was to *"Credere, obbedire, combattere"* ("To believe, to obey, to fight"). No Italian has ever done more damage to his fatherland than the one who proclaimed himself always right. He who urged his countrymen "to believe, to obey, to fight" coerced them to believe in the most absurd ideology, to fight toward ignominious defeat, and to obey in order to become serfs of Adolf Hitler.

Adopting the principle that no authority should be accepted without challenge by no means implies that one should not respect authority. A distinction must be made between the *authoritative* person—one who knows a great deal about a subject or who through circumstances has become especially wise and capable of understanding human needs and human anguish—and the *authoritarian* person—one who preaches certain concepts and actually seeks through demagogy to condition others to accept them merely in order to retain or increase his own power. Whereas the authoritative person increases the range of options available to his fellow men, the authoritarian one restricts other people's options. The disintegration that we see in our contemporary world has to some extent been brought on by an attitude of contempt for the authoritative and of ready compliance toward the authoritarian or by a combination of these two attitudes.

THE FEW AND THE MANY

We must now return to Abraham and to the request he made of God. Is the principle implied in his request, applicable and feasible? Should the virtue of a few compensate for the guilt of the multitude and be reason for forgiveness for all? This principle does not say that the guilt is erased or not to be accounted for, but that—in certain particular situations—it is to be forgiven.

This principle is certainly not a juridical one based on law. At first look, the principle seems to involve a number of large concepts, such as individual guilt, collective guilt (about which I shall say more later); individual goodness, collective goodness; guilt of the few versus goodness of the many, goodness of the few versus guilt of the many. Closer inspection reveals that in this case individual guilt is not bypassed, and that the issue of collective guilt does not fully operate. In Sodom and Gomorrah everyone except certain members of Lot's family is individually guilty. What is considered in chapter 19 of Genesis is the question whether individual merit or the merit of a few is enough to engender collective acquittal and forgiveness. God seems to accept this belief. He is willing to save the whole city if He finds ten righteous people.

Ten is a special number, of course; it is the number of the fingers on a person's hands, which fabricated civilization. And arithmetic is based on the number of fingers, which later inspired the decimal system. Ten is the *minyan*, the minimum number of men required to establish a Jewish community where religious services can be held. But of course the number ten should not be considered in its literal mathematical meaning. What the biblical episode probably refers to is whether in general the moral high stature of a small minority is sufficient reason to apply the principle of mercy to a whole community. We oftener pose a different question: can the little-known virtues of the many redeem the atrocious deeds of the few? Common criminals, but especially the great criminal political leaders, have inflicted brutality and suffering on large sections of humankind, but humanity has survived even these enormities. Even in periods of great brutality countless small good deeds performed by people have been able to overcome the tide of evil on a global scale. Criminals and psychopaths have, in most instances, been in a small minority, and the wicked and infamous leaders have been defeated by the soul of common man. Not always, to be sure. Although the terrible crimes of Nazism and fascism were conceived by only a handful of leaders, the cooperation, or at least the guilty acquiescence, of a large group of people was necessary to implement the crimes. Many people allowed themselves to be involved in complicity. Hitler may have been considered as powerful as a god; yet there was nobody to tell him, "Even if you think the Jews are sinners, aren't there among them fifty, forty-five, ten righteous? Are you going to destroy all of them?"

"All of them," would have been Hitler's answer. But the situation in any case was the reverse of the circumstances involving Abraham. It was Hitler's implicit intention to destroy the Jews not because they were bad but precisely because from a moral point of view they were good. They were the bearers of the torch of Abraham, the transmitters of the Bible, of the principle that—to paraphrase Zachariah —not might, nor power, but the spirit of God should be man's foremost concern.

Of course, in Germany, too, there was a minority of righteous people who fought Hitler. The Reverend Martin Niemoeller, who opposed the nazification of the Protestant church and rejected Nazi racial theories, is an example; and perhaps because of this dauntless minority Germany, too, was saved from the fate of Sodom and Gomorrah. A recurring theme in the Old Testament is that a small minority will benefit or will save the whole group—or the whole of mankind. Through Abraham and his seed—that is, Israel—"All the families of the earth will be blessed." And also when Israel errs or is defeated, a few will remain, like a few olives on an olive tree battered by a storm; a *sheerith*, a remnant, will remain; ten will form a new community which will support the Law of God, the moral law.

When political and cultural catastrophes have befallen mankind, there has always been a minority or an elite that has managed to save civilization. Through the ravages of the Middle Ages a small group of scholars saved what was great in the Greek-Roman world, and from what they preserved and rescued eventually came the Renaissance. Whenever disaster descends upon the masses, a dissenting minority survives with its integrity intact and remains the bearer of the torch of truth, goodness, and justice. I have called it an elite, though I do not mean to imply by this term our present-day sense of intellectual hubris or social pride. In the original French, *élite* means chosen by chance or by divine intervention—in the context of this discussion, chosen to perpetuate the idea of morality and justice.

The fact that God elects to doom Sodom and Gomorrah means that there is no elite, no saving minority in the two cities of evil. God wants to show Abraham that in the future there has to remain at least a saving remnant of the children of Israel in order to perpetuate the people, both physically and in their spiritual identity.

This is not to suggest that the deserving people will be saved and the others will not. Here we would have to confront another very difficult problem, which constitutes the main theme of Book of Job. The episode of Sodom and Gomorrah seems to imply that if the preservation of a group or an ideology depends on people, there must be at least a small minority who are capable of insuring that preservation. This point of view should not be taken merely as an ethical or a religious precept, for it is a fact susceptible of historical validation. Many times in history only the so-called opposition—an "idealistic fringe"—has protected the course of history from the errors of the mainstream. The Jewish people have always seen themselves in that minority position.

Abraham and his descendants do not aim, as Augustine later does, to attain the City of God. To so aim would mean a renunciation of the historical world, acceptance only of Heaven and rejection of earth—in a certain sense, the complete separation of spirit and matter. Abraham and his descendants are for interactionism. And God Himself is portrayed throughout the Old Testament in this way. "I am the Lord thy God who brought thee out of the land of Egypt." Action within the historical world is stressed again and again. "Remember that you were slaves in the land of Egypt." Over and over, we come upon the admonition to remember. People are to bear in mind, and to learn from, the lessons of history. "The stranger who sojourns among you has to be treated as you treat yourself."

The citizens of Sodom and Gomorrah pertain to this world; they are part of history but have removed any spiritual element from it. In a way they have given up their right to belong to mankind, the species that has capacity to choose between right and wrong. They no longer deserve to be part of future history. Could God spare Sodom and Gomorrah, though not even ten righteous men are there? In the biblical writings God is portrayed as very compassionate. However, to spare the city when not even the minimal saving minority exists would mean to condone crime. Because of his special position (on account of which "all the families of the earth should be blessed"), Abraham has to learn to teach "the way of the Lord, to do righteousness and justice." Crime cannot be condoned.

PUNISHMENT

If crime is not to be condoned, the meting out of punishment follows; punishment can also be seen as having a redemptive value. In the myth of Adam and Eve human beings show the capacity to degrade themselves, to choose the wrong alternative. Adam and Eve disobey God, but Cain does much worse. Because of envy he commits the first murder. (And since then many have imitated his example.) In

most of the Old Testament there seems to be a correspon-
dence between doing right and divine reward and between
wrongdoing and punishment. In the farewell Discourses of
Moses, in many Psalms and in many portions of the Prophets, acceptance of the Divine will is proposed out of pure
love of God and not because of interest in a reward. However, throughout the Discourses of Moses, as well as in other
biblical writings, material and historical reward for obedience and material and historical punishment for disobedi-
ence are strongly and frequently stressed. Being originally
concerned with the life of an agricultural people, the Bible
at first refers often to the rainfall, a bounty that is necessary
in the hot land of Canaan. But what begins as the gift of
rain and dew expands to include other benefits bestowed by
the magnanimity of God. However, especially in the Book
of Job, but also in Jeremiah, Habakkuk, some Psalms, and
Ecclesiastes, it is pointed out that the wicked may prosper
and the righteous may suffer. This historical fact, requir-
ing a much more profound and complicated analysis, will
be examined in chapter 4.

For now, it must be stated that, according to the Old
Testament, evil is not to be condoned, that it increases
greatly the distance between God and man, and that punishment is not only acceptable but necessary. Punishment
is not merely payment for wrongdoing but also has a pur-
ifying function. Several centuries later Plato is to reaffirm
this idea. In his dialogue Gorgias particularly, Plato defends
punishment. He not only reaffirms the biblical concept
that it is better to suffer injustice than to commit it, but he
also contends that the guilty one should seek to be judged
and punished just as a sick man should find a physician and
receive treatment.

The Bible and Plato are similar in their views of punishment. Two other concepts of punishment or penalty, however, have also prevailed in history, philosophy, and sociology. One theory goes back to Aristotle who, in the *Nichomachean Ethics*, states that the purpose of penalty is as much as possible to re-establish the order that is inherent in the sense of justice. At times it is not possible to achieve this order, but an effort must be made to do so. For instance, if A kills B, no matter how much A is punished, there will be no compensation for the loss of the life of B, but punishment should be inflicted to reduce the advantage that A had unjustly taken of B. A third concept of penalty, stressed especially by sociologists, considers punishment a social defense: the protection of society, the prevention of evil, by example, the re-establishment of feelings of solidarity among the citizens who do not transgress. These three major concepts of punishment are often intermingled; each considers punishment necessary and to an extent follows Abraham's God of history.

COLLECTIVE GUILT

As for collective guilt, can we say that in the Old Testament, in the episode of Sodom and Gomorrah and others, this concept is operative? Insofar as we can judge from the events of history, does collective guilt have any validity?

I believe that collective guilt is affirmed by the Bible and by secular history not as a substitute for individual guilt but as an additional human condition having characteristics of its own. Nor should collective guilt be confused with such religious doctrines as original sin or the unworthiness of man in the presence of God.

From a juridical standpoint collective guilt has no basis

whatsoever; the law cannot punish a group for a crime but must deal with the individual. Morally, the substitution of collective guilt for individual guilt is unacceptable as it would diminish or erase the individual's sense of personal responsibility by shifting the onus onto the collectivity; collective guilt is not the guilt of anyone in particular. Collective punishments have been inflicted on defeated nations or on labor unions that have gone on strike, but in these cases the implications have always been more social and political than ethical.

The following characteristics are generally valid for collective guilt: (1) it must be experienced in addition to individual guilt, not in place of it; (2) the retribution is generally expected to come from God, or from another collectivity, or from the course of history under the guidance of God. In addition to Sodom and Gomorrah, we may cite a few examples.

In the year 70 C.E. the Romans defeated the Jews, destroyed Jerusalem, committed atrocious barbarities, and on the ninth day of the month of Ab, according to the Jewish calendar, destroyed the Second Temple. The Roman Emperor rewarded the conquerors by donating to them lands and villas in the most beautiful part of Italy, near the Gulf of Naples, in Pompeii and Herculaneum. In the summer of the year 79, nine years later, almost to the day after the destruction of the Temple, a fate similar to that of Sodom and Gomorrah was reserved for these cruel and sacrilegious people. The eruption of the volcano Vesuvius buried all of them, together with the cities that had benefited from so unjust a war. And the Roman Empire fell, too, and so did all the nations or civilizations that had allowed decadence and corruption to prevail and evil to remain unpunished.

Abraham and the Contemporary Mind

In *The Rise and Fall of the City of Mahagonny*, the German playwright Bertolt Brecht portrays in modern form the fate of Sodom and Gomorrah. Mahagonny, a new city where the evil of the worst aspects of a bourgeois society prevails, is finally visited by God, and perishes.

Since ancient times collective guilt seems to result more from what the community neglects to do than from what it does. In other words, the omission is more important than the commission. In primitive communities the whole tribe considers itself responsible for the transgression of ritual and magic and expects to be punished in its totality. In the Bible, in the book of Jonah, the whole city of Nineveh is to be punished and destroyed, but instead the whole city atones, each individual as well as the collectivity, and is thus saved. Sophocles' *Oedipus Rex* refers also to collective guilt. Freud, like most readers of the famous play, focused on the personal guilt of the king, Oedipus; but in the play the whole city of Thebes is punished with a terrible plague, because the citizens have allowed the murder of King Laius to be forgotten. The crime has not been uncovered, and Laius's slayer is still unpunished.

The Germans actually guilty of having given the terrible orders to exterminate the Jews were relatively few in number; and, indeed, probably only a few thousand Germans implemented these orders. But many millions of Germans did not act to prevent the Nazi leaders and their henchmen from perpetrating their horrible crimes.

Few are the leaders who wage immoral wars, but many are the citizens who do not oppose such wars and at free elections vote for keeping the same leaders in power. Those who are aware of evil and do nothing to prevent it or to oppose it become, at first, watchers and, later, guardians of evil. Doing nothing to prevent or to oppose evil becomes evil itself.

REDEMPTION WITHIN HISTORY

Throughout the Old Testament redemption is shown as possible not only in Heaven but also on earth, in temporal and historical existence. No original sin prevents one from undergoing salvation on earth or after death.

Other religious thinkers have rather different views. For instance, Augustine considers Cain, who slew his brother Abel, the founder of the earthly city, the City of Man. Augustine asks himself why

> the good are chastised with the wicked, when God is pleased to visit with temporal punishments. . . . They are punished together, not because they have spent an equally corrupt life, but because the good as well as the wicked, though not equally with them, love this present life; while they ought to hold it cheap, that the wicked, being admonished and reformed by their example, might lay hold of the eternal.*

In the modern world, the elite as well as the people at large have generally hewed to the tradition of Abraham that the temporal and the earthly count, too. For a long time, especially in the Middle Ages, Augustinian views prevailed, especially among theologians and philosophers, but not in subsequent periods of history. Many great men have tried to help human beings during their temporary passage on earth—not only philosophers, like Jean-Jacques Rous-

* Augustine, *City of God* book 1, ch. 9.

seau, John Locke, and Immanuel Kant, but also a long line
of political leaders and social thinkers. Stressing the importance of the temporal has in many cases led to the neglect
of the spiritual and of the eternal values, but this neglect
is not implied in the interactionism that originated with
Abraham, the patriarch. Athens, Florence, Geneva, Paris,
London, San Francisco are not cities of God in the Augustinian sense, but they are also far from being Sodom and
Gomorrah.

Collective guilt, too, is susceptible to redemption. But if
it is not redeemed, it should more and more disturb man's
conscience. Often collective guilt consists, as I have already mentioned, of doing nothing to correct or to remedy
an evil already perpetrated by the collectivity to which
one belongs, or by the leader of the collectivity.

The Finnish psychiatrist Martti Siirala * feels that we
should feel guilty not only for the evil that we ourselves
have done, or have not prevented being done, or have not
remedied, but also for the evil that previous generations
have committed. Thus Americans should feel guilty for
what was done to the Indians and the black people. I per-
sonally believe that we should experience some collective
guilt for what previous generations did, but should feel
much more guilt because we have not sufficiently remedied
or corrected what was done in the past. It is our place and
duty to implement such remedies and the corrections whenever we are capable of doing so.

The importance that the Jewish religion gives to collective guilt as well as to collective redemption is demonstrated by the fact that many traditional prayers are for

---

* Martti Siirala, *Die Schizophrenie—des Einzeln und der Allgemein-
heit* (Gottingen: Vandenhoeck e Ruprecht, 1961); and "Schizophrenia:
A Human Situation," *American Journal of Psychoanalysis* (1963)
23:39–58.

the benefit of past generations and for the whole people of Israel. For instance, some prayers in the Yom Kippur service stupify non-Jews—and might also be used by anti-Semites to show how sinful the Jews admit to being. In these prayers Jews recite a litany of how they have cheated, murdered, stolen, and so forth. The meaning of this type of prayer is that among millions of Jews some may have been murderers, thieves, and so forth, and that everyone must pray for them. Jews assume a communal sense of responsibility because they have not been able to divert some of their fellows from evil. Thus, although one's major responsibility is for one's own actions, a person must also acknowledge some responsibility for what the collectivity does.

Alexander and Margarete Mitscherlich,* well-known German psychoanalysts, have described the inability of the German people to mourn for what their fellow citizens did during the Second World War. But the Mitscherliches' regret can be extended to the whole world; people in general have not been able to mourn adequately for the Armenian massacre, for the Holocaust, and for Hiroshima. We shall return to this important subject in chapter 4.

The lack of an adequate sense of collective guilt is generally itself accountable to collective entities, such as culture, social institutions, government, and enclaves of power. The individual may have only a dim view of his role in implementing or helping to perpetuate collective wrongdoing. Thus, because society sanctioned acts of injustice, many people did not feel guilty for owning slaves, discriminating against Jews and persecuting them, keeping minorities in an inferior state, and so forth.

Feelings of collective guilt would be completely elimi-

---

* Alexander Mitscherlich, and Margarete Mitscherlich, *The Inability to Mourn*, trans. B. R. Placzek (New York: Grove Press, 1975).

nated, and those of individual guilt strongly diminished, if the environment were to succeed in manipulating people completely, by means of conditioned reflexes, or operant conditioning, as Skinner describes and seems to advocate.* In a Skinnerian world, is there not only no freedom and dignity but no guilt. Skinner is partly right, however. To the extent that we allow society to mold us and to influence us to perform certain acts without individual choice and responsibility, we lose autonomy, and whatever guilt could still be felt would have to be collective.

But then why talk about guilt if it stems from social forces outside ourselves? First, the Skinnerian methods and other external influences are not totally effective in human beings. The ability to choose is greatly diminished but not completely eliminated. Eventually we have to rely on what is left of our individual capacity for guilt in order to remedy the collective guilt. Second, and most important, we are guilty of having allowed ourselves to become victims of collective guilt. Although the social forces were very strong, they were not so strong as irremediably to overwhelm our psyche in its totality. We have permitted ourselves to be channeled into the easier path. We have allowed these social forces to submerge our will and, in some cases, to lead us to act as Pavlovian dogs, not as human beings.

* B. F. Skinner, *Beyond Freedom and Dignity* (New York: Alfred A. Knopf, 1971).

CHAPTER

IV

The Binding of Isaac

William Tell (anonymous nineteenth-century wood engraving)

We come now to the most difficult part of the biblical story of Abraham, the episode called in the Jewish tradition the Akedah, or the binding of Isaac—called by others the sacrifice of Isaac.

Down through the centuries the episode has stirred people's imagination. On becoming acquainted with the story for the first time, one is struck with astonishment and trepidation. A person who has heard the story many times remains bewildered, wavering between accepting it as told or interpreting it, between focusing on a part of it or gauging what one senses is a still-to-be-explored profundity; but one's soul does not remain hungry.

Referring to the "Sacrifice of Isaac" Elie Wiesel writes,

> Terrifying in content, it has become a source of consolation to those who, in retelling it, make it part of their own experience. Here is a story that contains Jewish destiny in its totality, just as the flame is contained in the single spark by which it comes to life. Every major theme, every passion and obsession that make Judaism the adventure that it is, can be traced back to it.*

If throughout the centuries no interpretation given to this biblical story has appeared complete or final, must one conclude that the story is an absurd myth, comparable

* Elie Wiesel, *Messengers of God* (New York: Random House, 1976).

to the pagan story of Pallas Athena, born from the forehead of Zeus, or of Aphrodite, born from the foam of the sea? Can the binding of Isaac be just another myth in which what is to be noted today is some fantasy of the Ancients or at most the intricacies of a metaphor? The answer is that the resonance and the mystery of the Abraham episode put it in a class by itself. A person raised in the Judeo-Christian tradition always senses in this story the impact of some truth that nevertheless continues to be elusive. This episode is not the only example of a story in the Bible evoking great perplexity and awe. The Book of Job is only slightly less difficult to understand. We must then assume that we are entitled to search for a truth.

Another question: if through the centuries the greatest theologians, rabbis, and scholars have not succeeded in interpreting fully the meaning of the story, is it not a piece of hubris for me to assume that I can succeed? Indeed, it would be were I to claim the ability to grasp the elusive meaning in its totality. My aim is humble. I want to continue the search, not knowing where it will take me. I remind myself of what I said in chapter 1: salient passages of the Bible confront us not with a clear and distinct presentation but rather with an "open statement" that can be interpreted again and again. The incomplete understanding often adds intensity to the myth. What is absent in our understanding is present as a hope of an enlightenment to come, as an urge to continue the search.

The story of the Akedah is found in chapter 22 of Genesis. God calls Abraham and tests him. According to the tradition,* Abraham is tested ten times, and the binding of Isaac is the last and most difficult test. Whereas Abraham passes his test successfully, we who have to pass

---

* Avoth, V, 4.

the test of interpreting it are forced to settle for a partial and hypothetical accomplishment.

God said to Abraham, "Take, I pray thee, thy son, thine only son Isaac, whom thou lovest, and get into the land of Moriah, and offer him for a burnt offering upon one of the mountains which I tell thee of. And Abraham rose early in the morning" and proceeded with the intention of inplementing God's order.

But how is this possible? How can God request so much of a loving father? How can a loving father agree to the request, even if it has come from God? Is God requesting the sacrifice of a human life? Will Abraham become a murderer if he follows God's request? And how strange, indeed, that the man who argues with God in an attempt to save the two cities of sinners, Sodom and Gomorrah, so submissively agrees to this most painful request! What does all this mean?

No doubt everybody who wants to interpret the story experiences an inner turmoil that is difficult to quiet. How can God ask so much? How can Abraham be willing to give so much? And what about the ethics of God's demand? And the ethics of Abraham's willingness to follow?

While it is impossible to review here all the explanations given by various authors; I shall consider a few salient ones before advancing my own views.

EMIL FACKENHEIM'S INTERPRETATION AND ITS DERIVATIVES

Emil Fackenheim has helped us to understand how Immanuel Kant would interpret the binding of Isaac episode, and has added how he—Fackenheim—would differ from

Kant. According to Kant, the whole evolution of the episode is wrong. First, a real moral act must be autonomous, not heteronomous: that is, it must originate with the person who implements it, not from an external source; and even an order imposed by God is an external source. The person must will to do the moral act. He is also the maker of the law that will lead him to perform the moral act. If Abraham follows the will of God, and not his own will, he is not free; his action is heteronomous. Fackenheim asks the following question:

> How can man appropriate a God-given law or commandment, accepting and performing it as though it were his own, while yet remaining, in the very act of appropriation, essentially and receptively related to its divine giver? How can a man *morally* obey a law that is, and never ceased to be, essentially revealed? *

Fackenheim attempts to solve his question by stating that the human being is a free agent, even when he receives a command from God, for he can accept or reject such a command. The choice is his.

For Fackenheim, then, true freedom is a freely chosen response to a divine call; that is the way, in his view, that the concept of autonomy in Judaism differs from that in Kant. But Fackenheim himself gets into other troubles. How can God command the sacrifice of Isaac, when Judaism so much values human life in the here and now? Fackenheim asks, Why does the Jew revere Abraham when, like Kant, every Jew considers child sacrifice to be forbidden? He answers;

* Emil Fackenheim, *Encounters between Judaism and Modern Philosophy* (New York: Basic Books, 1973).

Because of *a perpetual reenacted radical surprise*. Kant's "common reason" rules out all surprise when it affirms the intrinsic value of humanity to be absolute. To receive the Torah on account of Abraham's merit is, first, to have called all things into question in the sight of the Divinity, the intrinsic value of humanity included; second, it is to accept that some things are in question no longer; and, third, it is to receive, in surprise as well as gratitude, the value of humanity as a gift that the Divinity might have withheld and that is yet given forever.*

Fackenheim seems to me difficult to understand. If I interpret him correctly, he implies that the end justifies the means. Because of what Abraham does, God makes a covenant with him, and the value of humanity is recognized forever. This point of view seems to me, again, not to be in conformity with the Kantian principle according to which humanity is seen as an end in itself and not as a means. "Act so as to use humanity, whether in your own person or in the person of another, always as an end, never as merely a means." But Isaac, if sacrificed, would be a means. According to Kant "the categorical imperative" or moral law must be autonomous, not heteronomous; it must come only from one's good will. God's intervention not only is not necessary but would disturb its autonomy.

And yet Kant formulates another principle for the moral act, the principle of universality. "Act in conformity with that maxim and that maxim only, which you can at the same time will to be a universal law." Actions should spring not from individual situations or personal tendencies and desires, but only from principles that can be universalized. But can the human being really arrogate to himself the right to universalize? Kant gives the example of a man

* Ibid., pp. 69–70; italics, Fackenheim's.

who, after a series of misfortunes, contemplates suicide. When he contemplates applying his plan to mankind, he realizes that this plan is wrong. If everybody were to commit suicide, humanity would perish. But this is not a good example. Kant confuses "everybody" with "anyone who underwent a series of tragic misfortunes" or even with "people who underwent tragic misfortunes" with intensity similar or approximating those of the man he takes as an example. There are, thus, already three different categories in his example, and more can be found. I know of someone whose suicide I cannot criticize. Giuseppe Iona, president of the Jewish congregation of Venice, committed suicide rather than give the Nazis the list of Venetian Jews. Nor would any of us be willing to criticize the suicide committed by the besieged Jews in Masada.

Not to kill is another so-called categorical imperative, but soldiers are instructed to kill in the battlefield. Not to lie is yet another such imperative, but doctors lie when they feel a patient is not able to accept the truth, or when it would be detrimental to him to know the truth. Psychiatrists often withhold a truth until a patient is able to face it. In some cases that ability may never be attained. I suppose that if unfortunate or evil circumstances did not exist, it would be easy to formulate universal maxims.

It seems to me that in order to formulate principles of universal validity, man has to search for God's guidance and ask himself what God would want, so that his action could have the value of a universal ethical fact. If someone is not able to ask for such guidance, he must search for the absolute validity of what he is trying to do; but to search for an absolute validity is equivalent to searching for God, even if one does not believe or cannot conceptualize a personal God. In fact, the attribute "absolute" pertains only to God or to what we conceive as divine.

In summary, it is true that we cannot see ethical value in the Akedah if we accept Kant's ethical theory. However, it is also difficult to accept Kant's idea of the universality of the categorical imperative unless we accept a concept of God. But if we accept a concept of God, we can believe that God, too, may suggest—indeed, request—exceptions to the imperative.

KIERKEGAARD AND THE STORY OF THE AKEDAH

The flourishing of existential philosophy in the last few decades has brought about a revival of Kierkegaard, who is deservedly considered to be one of its greatest masters. With this revival the attention of many has focused on his book *Fear and Trembling*, in which, taking as a paradigm the story of the sacrifice of Isaac, he expresses the theory of the teleological suspension of the ethical. Kierkegaard affirms that a man who has true faith in God may neglect the established principles of ethics and obey the Divine call. That is what Abraham, the knight of faith, as Kierkegaard calls him, does. There are two sets of principles: ethical and religious. The ethical is comprehensible to all men; that is what Kant calls the universal. The religious by nature is private or particular to a specific human being and is not understood by others. The right man must love the ethical. The fact that he loves it, gives him the right to suspend it—and to suspend it only if, and when, he does so in obedience to God's command. When he acts in this way, he follows the "religious set."

Kierkegaard's conception has found welcome in Protestant circles and also among some Jewish thinkers. Fackenheim certainly prefers Kierkegaard's view on this matter to Kant's. Jacob Haley, too, has a high regard for Kierkegaard's interpretation and believes that Kierkegaard's suspension of the ethical is one of the "core" concepts of rabbinical thinking. In the case of Abraham, a higher imperative, the faith in God, permitted a violation of the principles of ethical life.

This interpretation is intriguing and yet difficult to accept. God as conceived in the Judeo-Christian tradition cannot recommend a suspension of the ethical.

THEORIES CONCERNING CHILD SACRIFICE

Many interpretations, repeatedly formulated with little variation by various authors over the years, see in the story of the Akedah only Judaism's opposition to child sacrifice —a practice quite common in ancient times, especially with people among whom the Hebrews sojourned. It is correct to affirm that the Bible condemns child sacrifice, but this fact is not the most pertinent aspect of the story. For some of these commentators the Abraham-Isaac episode is representative of that period in history when human sacrifice was replaced by animal sacrifice.

But child sacrifice has after all been outlawed for a long time, and yet the Abraham-Isaac story maintains its great spiritual value today. If the episode dealt only with the report or even condemnation of a rite practiced in ancient times, it would retain at most only anthropological interest. Robert Gordis,* although rejecting the notion that the episode depicts opposition to child sacrifice, provides an explanation similarly difficult to accept. According to Gordis, in "the background of Oriental religion as a whole, there is no suspension of the ethical involved in God's request." Gordis writes that "the sacrifice of a child was an all-but-universal practice in ancient Semitic religion and beyond." At the time of the prophet Micah this practice was viewed with horror, but "Abraham, living nearly a thousand years before Micah in a world permeated by pagan religion, did not feel himself confronted by a moral crisis when he was commanded by God to sacrifice Isaac, and he proceeded to obey." But the fact that the story may have some historical basis does not explain its full spiritual and symbolic meaning. As I have discussed in chapter 1, a story maintains great value for us precisely because it transcends whatever historical basis it happens to have. What requires analysis is whether in different historical milieus, including our own today, we can consider Abraham's conduct ethical, unethical, or the result of a suspension of ethics, and as having other meanings beyond the ethical aspect of God's request and Abraham's compliance.

WELLISCH'S PSYCHOANALYTIC THEORY

Psychoanalytic theories of biblical episodes have appeared in the literature from time to time; the best known psychoanalytic study of the Akedah is by Erich Wellisch, pub-

*Robert Gordis, "The Faith of Abraham: A Note on Kierkegaard's 'Teological Suspension of the Ethical,'" *Judaism* (1976) 25:414–19.

lished in 1954. Dr. Erich Wellisch was a Viennese psychiatrist who left Austria in 1938 and settled in England. It was his belief that science and religion should become unified, and he devoted himself to the study and development of biblical psychology. Unfortunately he died while his best-known work, *Isaac and Oedipus,** was being printed.

In the conclusion to his book he writes that, according to the biblical view, he accepts

> the Akedah Motif, as the result of Divine intervention, developed suddenly in history, at a definite time and place and in definite circumstances. Before this historic event a gradual development of Akedah tendencies among all nations of the world prepared the way for the full Akedah experience.

According to Wellisch the "Akedah motif" is a solution, or rather the full solution, of the Oedipus complex, first described by Freud. However, Wellisch does not focus on what Freud considers the main point of the complex—the rivalry and subsequent hatred that in early childhood the son has for his father (or the daughter for her mother)—but on the rivalry and hatred that the father has for the son (or the mother for the daughter). Again using Greek mythology, he calls this relationship the "Laius complex." He supports the frequency (perhaps the universality) of the Laius complex in two ways. First, he gives historical evidence for the common practice of infanticide in primitive times and in primitive cultures. He writes,

> The fact that infanticide once was a general custom amongst practically all races and nations is a shocking discovery. Many reasons can be given for this sinister fact but all can

*Erich Wellisch, *Isaac and Oedipus* (London: Routledge & Kegan Paul, 1956).

be reduced to that of selfishness of the parents. Parenthood involves personal sacrifices for the sake of the child, and indeed, the whole human family.

Although he mentions infanticide committed by mothers, too, Wellisch focuses on that committed by fathers. According to him, the main motive for infanticide by fathers was "unwillingness to give up their absolute superiority for the benefit of the growing children and particularly the eldest son."

Echoing Freud's *Totem and Taboo*, Wellisch writes that the patriarchal leader feared that "he would be overthrown, ousted from his possession and lose his leadership." More disturbing was the father's fear of being outmatched by his son in the possession of his wives, in a situation where "incestuous wishes of the son towards his own mother and his desire to possess other wives of his father's class were a terrible reality. . . . The greatest danger was the possibility that the son, in order to achieve leadership and possession of women, would kill the father." In primitive times patricide was common, but less common than infanticide. Infanticide was a prevention against patricide, but was often rationalized with the belief that the gods demanded it and were pleased by it. Thus, infanticide was not murder but a virtuous deed, a sacrifice that would cleanse the parents of their sins. Conscious or unconscious wishes about infanticide persisted in ancient times (and persist even today); but, according to Wellisch, Abraham solves them with the episode of the Akedah. Wellisch believes that "until Abraham the father's authority was based on fear. Since Abraham it has been based on love." The order from God is experienced as an introjected injunction that leads to Abraham's formation of a full superego. At the same time that unconsciously Abraham experiences aggressive tendencies toward Isaac, consciously he experiences pain and anguish.

Wellisch elaborates his theory by stating that after the binding of Isaac a fundamental change takes place in Abraham, "*a turning of mind* which divided the history of the world into two parts: one before and one after the Akedah" (Italics in the original). Abraham realizes that God demands life and not death. Wellisch feels that Abraham rejects the former dominance of what Freud calls the death instinct, and entirely abandons his aggressive tendencies against Isaac. Abraham thus changes from a potentially destructive parent to an all-loving parent, and this love first directed toward Isaac was amplified to include all human beings—not only his contemporaries but future generations. According to Wellisch God, too, changes, at least in name. Whereas at the beginning of the story He is called Elohim, at the end He is called by the ineffable name with which thereafter He will be referred to by the Hebrews. Wellisch supports his theories with some clinical data derived from psychiatric practice, some of which he reports in his book. The data deal with patients, children whom he examined in his capacity as medical director of Grayford Child Guidance Clinic in Kent. These children had psychological difficulties because of the neurotic aggressive tendencies of their fathers. Eventually with the help of psychotherapy the fathers understood the nature of the problem, and the children improved or recovered. A psychotherapeutic Akedah took place.

Nobody can doubt Wellisch's sincerity and devotion to his work. He attempts a harmonious fusion of his psychiatric-psychoanalytic training and experience with his Jewish heritage. Whether he succeeds in telling us something new and convincing, is another question. It is true that infanticide was common in certain societies and in some societies is still common today. It is also true that in psychiatric practice we find many children and adolescents whose conflicts originate in their relations with their fathers. However, to fit all this in the Akedah story seems difficult. Even if Abraham has aggressive tendencies toward Isaac which he is able to overcome at a time when he internalizes the command given by God through the Angel, "Lay not thy hand on the lad," Wellisch offers no psychological explanation of how this change comes about. He tells us that human history is divided into two parts at the moment of this unique and unprecedented event. But he does not explain psychologically how that moment comes to be.

Wellisch's interpretation is another version of the theory that the Akedah represents a revolt against the practice of infanticide. It is presented in psychoanalytic terminology and as a derivative of the Oedipus complex, but it offers nothing new.

Many authors, psychoanalysts and nonpsychoanalysts alike, argue that the Oedipus complex is not a universal phenomenon. But even if one accepts the Oedipus complex as a universal phenomenon, occurring at least in altered forms and not in accordance with the typical Freudian formulations, one finds it difficult to accept as universal the Laius complex and the tendency to infanticide. The human race would not have survived.

In this book Wellisch mentions several cases of child sacrifice or attempted sacrifice that are famous in the legends of various peoples. In one of them, On, King of Sweden, slaughters nine of his sons in the belief that he can prolong his life. He is about to kill Egil, his tenth son, but Egil is rescued by the Swedes and becomes king. According to Wellisch, Egil only half-heartedly resists his father's request that he die. Later, in a fight with a bull that, according to Wellisch, is a symbolic image of his father, Egil dies.

Better known is the attempted sacrifice of Iphigenia, as reported in Greek mythology. The goddess Artemis, offended, is preventing the Greek fleet from sailing during the Trojan expedition. When it is announced that Artemis can only be appeased by the sacrifice of King Agamemnon's daughter Iphigenia, the king, after turbulent inner conflict, agrees, and witnesses the tragic rite, although hiding his face. At the last moment Artemis mercifully intervenes and carries Iphigenia away to a temple in Tauris.

These myths, and other similar ones, lack the intense spirituality of the Abraham-Isaac episode. A would-be sacrifice of a son that is somewhat less remote spiritually from the Abraham-Isaac episode and that Wellisch does not mention, is that of William Tell's son.

The story of William Tell has played an important role in Swiss folklore and in the legendary accounts of Switzerland's past. Skeptical historians have relegated the story to the realm of fable; but according to the Swiss historian Georg Thürer, some details of the narrative, as transmitted through several generations, "are now known to have a firm historical foundation." *

According to the story, in the thirteenth century the Swiss patriot William Tell refuses obeisance and homage to the tyrant Gessler. As punishment he is forced to shoot an apple off his son's head. Since nobody thinks that he will master the arduous deed, especially under the stress of the emotional upheaval, this is tantamount to a command that

---

*Georg Thürer, *Free and Swiss. The Story of Switzerland*, trans. R. P. Heller and E. Long (London: Oswald Wolff, 1970).

Tell sacrifice his son. But Tell does succeed; his son is saved. The almost miracle leads eventually to an uprising against tyranny, to the killing of Gessler, and to freedom for all. The story entered literature with Schiller's drama *William Tell* in 1804, and music with Rossini's opera *William Tell* in 1829.

DAVID POLISH'S INTERPRETATION

In a beautiful book, *The Eternal Dissent* *—which has inspired me in many ways, and from which I have learned a great deal, but which I cannot accept in its entirety— Rabbi David Polish advances a genuinely new interpretation of the Abraham-Isaac episode. According to Polish, the mistake made repeatedly in interpreting this event derives from the fact that many authors begin their analysis with chapter 22 of Genesis, and not earlier. He believes that "an important though glossed-over answer is to be found before our eyes, hidden because it is so apparent, evasive because it is unconcealed." The rabbis, too, he tells us, sense that the interpretation is to be found in antecedent events.

Like many other stories in the Bible, this opens with these words, "And it came to pass after these things." What things? These words always refer to antecedent events that have a bearing upon the episode to be narrated.

The clue has to be found in the previous story of Abraham and Ishmael, where Abraham submits to Sarah's request and chases his son Ishmael away. It is true that Ish-

* David Polish, *The Eternal Dissent* (London: Abelard-Schuman, n.d.).

mael is given to violence, that God suggests to Abraham that he comply with Sarah's demand, and that He makes it clear to Abraham that Ishmael, too, will be the founder of a great nation. Nevertheless, driving Ishmael out is very difficult for Abraham to do. The Midrash calls this chasing away of Ishmael the ninth test of Abraham. Polish sees Abraham's obedience to God in the Akedah episode as an atonement for his guilt, derived from having agreed to Sarah's request to expell Ishmael. Abraham's acquiescence to God in the Isaac episode is interpreted as expiation for his earlier acquiescence to Sarah. Abraham does not want to send Ishmael away; he loves him. (And yet the rabbis were to classify him a rapist, a murderer, and an idolater.) Polish writes that "only by reliving with Isaac what he experienced with Ishmael will expiation come." Polish adds in a sort of conclusion,

> Now, by joining the Ishmael and Isaac stories into a single narrative we learn that the *Akedah* is not only an account of unprotesting obedience and implicit faith of a test in submissiveness to God. It is rather a lesson in the grappling of Abraham, of the Jewish soul, with evil, and expiating it with all of one's powers, even with the child of one's loins and love. The test is not so much of Abraham's loyalty to God but of his capacity (by recognizing that banishment to the desert must be inexorably followed by binding on the mountain top) to push back the black tide of evil which he had once allowed to engulf him.

It is true that writers of the Bible apparently did not want to portray as perfect Abraham, or any other man—including Moses.

Now Abraham must experience guilt on account of his acquiescence in the expulsion of Ishmael; but if he were to agree to kill Isaac for what he did to Ishmael—who is after all not killed but lives to become the founder of a great nation—that guilt would be excessive, neurotic, and probably unconscious. Of course, feelings of this kind are possible. Abraham may experience excessive neurotic guilt, of which he is to a large extent unconscious. But even if this explanation is correct (and probably to some extent it is) Abraham's neurotic guilt hardly explains the meaning that the episode has come to have. I believe that here Rabbi Polish makes the kind of mistake more frequently made by my colleagues the psychoanalysts than by rabbis. When psychoanalysts look for the motivation behind great works of art or the acts of great men in history, they find it in a neurotic, often unconscious mechanism, related to some previous situation in the family context. The finding of neurotic motivation for the works of Leonardo, Michelangelo, Shakespeare, and Beethoven, is only one approach to the problem, important perhaps, but offering no guidance to the central concern in the evaluation of an aesthetic work or of a political event. The fact that Beethoven was neurotically motivated to write the Ninth Symphony neither adds nor detracts from the sublimity of the music. Nor does my knowledge that Beethoven had such neurotic motivation help me to understand the music aesthetically, or to see how that motivation was transformed into an acoustic expression of the highest spirituality. A similar argument is valid for religious events and myths. As I said in chapter 1, the usual psychoanalytic interpretation of a myth or of a historical event—even when correct—does not throw light on the *value* of the event. Uncovering a myth's primitive origin does not enlighten as to the import of the myth. Just as a strict factual historical account of an event does not reach its metaphysical meaning, so a psychoanalytic interpretation does not reach the philosoph-

ical, metaphysical or aesthetic value of whatever is creative in the outcome. No leap is made or even attempted.
It seems obvious to me that the biblical test, although not
wanting to portray Abraham as perfect, does not, on the
other hand, want to stress Abraham's guilt concerning Ishmael; otherwise, this concern would be explicitly expressed, as it is in other biblical passages. Abraham's test
is not an expiation. If a potential expiation is implied, this
potentiality remains to be investigated.

AUTHOR'S VIEWS OF THE AKEDAH

A rereading of chapter 22 of Genesis is in order. Then we
shall examine each part separately, and finally we shall try
to draw some conclusions.

> After these things God tested Abraham, and said to him,
> "Abraham!" And he said "Here am I." He said "Take, I beg
> you, thy son, thine only son Isaac, whom thou lovest and
> go to the land of Moriah, and offer him there for a burnt-
> offering upon one of the mountains which I tell thee of.
> So Abraham rose early in the morning, and saddled his
> ass, and took two of his young men with him, and Isaac, his
> son; and he cleaved the wood for the burnt-offering, and
> rose up, and went into the place of which God had told
> him.
> On the third day Abraham lifted up his eyes and saw the
> place afar off. Then Abraham said to his young men, "Stay
> here with the ass; I and the lad will go yonder and worship,
> and come again to you." And Abraham took the wood of
> the burnt offering, and laid it on Isaac his son; and he took
> in his hand the fire and the knife. So they went both of
> them together.
> And Isaac said to his father Abraham "My father!" And

he said "Here am I, my son." He said, "Behold, the fire and the wood, but where is the lamb for a burnt offering?" Abraham said, "God will provide himself the lamb for a burnt offering, my son." So they went both of them together.

When they came to the place of which God had told him, Abraham built an altar there, and laid the wood in order, and bound Isaac his son, and laid him on the altar, upon the wood. Then Abraham put forth his hand, and took the knife to slay his son. But the Angel of the Lord called to him from heaven, and said "Abraham, Abraham!" And he said "Here am I." He said "Lay not thy hand upon the lad, neither do thou anything to him, for now I know that thou lovest Me, and thou hast not withheld thy son, thy only son, from me."

And Abraham lifted up his eyes, and looked, and behold, behind him was a ram, caught in a thicket by his horns; and Abraham went and took the ram, and offered him up for a burnt-offering in the stead of his son. So Abraham called the name of that place The Lord will provide; as it is said to this day. "On the mount of the Lord it shall be provided."

And the Angel of the Lord called unto Abraham a second time out of heaven and said "By myself I have sworn —says the Lord, because thou has done this thing and hast not withheld thy son, thy only son, I will bless thee, and I will multiply thy descendants as the stars of heaven and as the sand which is on the seashore. And thy descendants shall possess the gate of their enemies, and by thy descendants shall all the nations of the earth bless themselves, because thou hast obeyed my voice." So Abraham returned to his young men, and they arose and went together to Beer-Sheba; and Abraham dwelt at Beer-sheba.*

To begin our analysis: "After these things . . ." Which things? Everything we know about Abraham: his relation

---

* Verses 20–24 of chapter 22 of Genesis are not reported here, as they do not refer to the Abraham-Isaac episode.

with the imageless God, the fact that God has told him to leave his country, his kindred, and his father's house and to go where God will direct him; the fact that God promises Abraham to make of him a great nation, to bless him, and to bless those who will bless him, and to bless all the families of the earth through him. Also Abraham's dealings with Lot, God's covenant with Abram, Abraham's defense of Sodom and Gomorrah, Abraham's relations with Sarah, Hagar, and Ishmael.

If one can assign relative weights to events, the most important is God's covenant with Abraham in chapter 17.

> Behold, my covenant is with you, and you shall be the father of a multitude of nations. No longer shall your name be Abram, but your name shall be Abraham; for I have made you the father of a multitude of nations. I will make you exceedingly fruitful; and I will make nations of you, and kings shall come forth from you. And I will establish my covenant between me and you and your descendants after you throughout their generations for an everlasting covenant, to be God to you and to your descendants after you.

"After these things," God calls Abraham in chapter 22, and he replies, "Here am I." And three times, Abraham replies, "Here am I," each time showing his readiness to receive a great message. And three messages he does receive. The first one is from God, the highest possible voice, but the voice that makes the most unexpected, most shocking request. The second one is the voice of Isaac, the voice of love. The third time is the voice of the Angel who reveals to Abraham the best possible solution. Abraham replies, "Here am I," to each of the three calls. Is he a passive protagonist in an intense drama with four characters: God, Isaac, the Angel, and Abraham? There is no passivity in Abraham. Each question must cause great activity in his soul: tremendous conflict, unpredicted turmoil, and immense pain. God urges Abraham to follow His request; He urges him by using the human term, "I beg thee." It is important to God that Abraham pass the test in consideration of the terrible tasks that Abraham's descendants will have to sustain through the centuries.

When we read that Abraham rises early in the morning and saddles his ass, we know that he has decided to go along with God's request.

Does he "suspend ethics"—Kierkegaard's euphemism for saying that Abraham becomes unethical? If we consider the episode from the point of view of Kantian ethics, Abraham does become unethical. (See pages 132–34.) But we have seen the contradictions of Kantian ethics in the framework of Jewish ethics. If a maxim reaches an absolute, universal validity, we need the concept of God to be sure of that validity. But if we accept the concept of God and we believe in God, we can accept the fact that God is requesting an exception. We have also seen that even the most ethical people sometimes make an exception to the Kantian categorical imperative. It is important in this regard also to mention Aristotle's concept of equity. Equity is "a correction of the law where it is defective on account of its universality." * In the formulation of universal laws it is impossible to foresee and make provision for every circumstance.

Similarly, although it is true—and here Jewish ethics is in agreement with Kantian ethics—that we should "act so as to use humanity, whether in your own person or in the person of another, always as an end, never as merely a means," this law, too, is susceptible of exceptions. Through-

*Aristotle, *Nichomachean Ethics* 1137, b.

out history people have used others or themselves for the sake of great ideals or missions. Hardly have such people been called unethical.

But given the fact that Abraham does not respond to a Kantian categorical imperative, can he nevertheless be sure that what God requests him to do is not unethical? Why does Abraham go ahead with the plan? Abraham is motivated by great faith in God. Every commentator has stressed his faith. Kierkegaard beautifully calls Abraham "the Knight of Faith." Saint Paul, too, in the Epistle to the Romans, celebrates Abraham's faith.

> What then shall we say about Abraham, our forefather according to the flesh? For if Abraham was justified by works, he has something to boast about, but not before God. For what does the Scripture say? "Abraham believed God, and it was reckoned to him as righteousness. Now to one who works, his wages are not reckoned as a gift but as his due." *

> In hope he [Abraham] believed against hope, that he should become the father of many nations; as he had been told "So shall your descendants be." He did not weaken in faith when he considered his own body which was as good as dead because he was about a hundred years old, or when he considered the barrenness of Sarah's womb. No distrust made him waver concerning the promise of God, but he grew strong in his faith as he gave glory to God, fully convinced that God was able to do what he had promised. That is why his faith was "reckoned to his as righteousness." †

Paul celebrates Abraham's faith but refers only to those acts of faith performed before Abraham was circumcised. Thus Paul does not mention the faith that Abraham demon-

---

* Romans 4:1–4.
† Romans 4:18–22.

strates in the Akedah, which occurs many years after his circumcision.

The faith of Abraham is beyond question. Perhaps, as Rabbi Ignaz Maybaum* suggests, trust is a better word than faith, if by trust is meant firm belief or confidence in the integrity, the reliability, the justice, and the goodness of whomever is trusted. According to Franz Rosenzweig,† trust is "the seed from which grow faith, hope and love."

Abraham who has become aware of the One Transcendent Imageless God, Abraham who has had so many encounters with God, has faith that, in spite of perplexing and disturbing appearances, whatever God suggests will be good, ethical, and aimed at a noble purpose. However, the same God who has promised him to make of Abraham a great nation—as a matter of fact, to make him become the father of a multitude of nations—and of course the same God who has indicated that all this will come about through the progeny of Abraham's son Isaac, is asking him now to sacrifice his only son. How can that be? If his only son will not live to become a father, how can the previous promises be fulfilled? Abraham feels sure that God will keep His promises, and therefore he believes that everything in the end will turn out well. But how can he be sure, after God has requested that he sacrifice Isaac? This sacrifice will be tantamount to a cancellation of the previous promises. Great, therefore, must be Abraham's faith, and great must be his doubt—both originating from God. And great is Abraham for his faith, and great is he for his doubt. For his doubt, too, because if he had only faith, the state of faith would put him in a state of certi-

---

* Ignaz Maybaum, *The Sacrifice of Isaac* (London: Vallentine, Mitchell, 1959).

† Quoted by Maybaum in *The Sacrifice of Isaac*. The quotation is from Franz Rosenzweig's *Der Stern der Erlösung*.

tude which would require no test, no conflict. The faith, though, is much greater than the doubt. We can assume that he has elements of doubt, but even elements of doubt are enough to make the test difficult when so much is at stake—"the only son, whom he loved." We can also assume that along with faith Abraham experiences a sense of mystery, but of a mystery that in spite of its mysteriousness is capable of being comprehended eventually. In this respect he reminds us of a fellow Jew, another great Jew who lived between three and four thousand years after Abraham: Albert Einstein. Einstein said on one occasion, "Mystery is its comprehensibility." These words imply faith, a religious faith, that everything can be comprehended. Part of the phenomenon of mysteriousness, in fact, relies on its being meaningful and susceptible sooner or later of being understood:

"And Isaac said to his father Abraham, "My father." And he said, "Here am I, my son," ready to answer this voice of love. When Isaac told him that he saw the fire and the wood, but not the lamb for the burnt offering, Abraham said "God will provide himself the lamb for a burnt offering, my son."

Is Abraham lying? Does he lie, as we know that some doctors do at times, in order not to frighten the patient? Although we have seen (p. 134) that lying is permitted in certain exceptional circumstances, and that we do not have to follow a Kantian categorical imperative concerning it, I do not believe he is lying; nor do I believe he thinks he is lying. His faith that God will provide makes his words to be expression of an act of faith and not of a lie. A similar evaluation can be made of what he says to the two young men who go along. "I and the lad will go yonder and worship, and come again to you." He says the truth.

"So they went both of them together." This sentence is repeated twice, in the sixth and the eighth paragraphs. Father and son go together on the mountain. In spite of God's terrifying request an atmosphere of calm pervades the whole episode. If fear exists, it is that fear of God which has a special meaning in the Bible; but there is no trembling. Maybaum is right in saying that Kierkegaard's title *Fear and Trembling* is inappropriate in relation to the Akedah. No trembling, terror, anguish, *angst*, is apparent once Abraham has agreed to follow God's request.

The third time Abraham says, "Here am I" is in answer to the Angel who brings him the message from God. "Now I know that thou lovest me, and thou hast not withheld thy son, thy only son, from me." We shall return to these words later. The Angel speaks again a second time as the messenger of God and reaffirms God's determination to multiply Abraham's descendants as the stars of heaven and as the sand which is on the seashore. God also reaffirms that by Abraham's descendants shall all the nations of the earth bless themselves. To this point, too, we shall return later.

Whereas at the beginning of the episode God enters as the one who will suggest the terrible task, at the end He has the Angel twice reveal His good message. He does not speak directly to Abraham. Why? We can only speculate. We can think that once the great test is successfully passed, God does not need to intervene directly. However, let us remember that at the beginning of the episode, although God Himself presents Abraham with the fearful request, He says, "I beg thee." He speaks like a man; He seems to beseech, to implore Abraham to follow His instructions, so important it is to Him that Abraham pass the test. Another possibility is that although God has found that Abraham has complete faith and love for Him, He does not want to confound him with a direct confrontation after having demanded so much. In acting through an intermediary, God wants to respect Abraham's human dignity.

Of the four characters in the great drama of the Akedah, the two main ones are God and Abraham. Isaac and the Angel play less important roles. The Angel is, of course, only an emissary of God. But Isaac's role again must be seen in a different light. He, too, is not just a passive, innocent would-be victim. He asks his father the dramatic question, "Where is the lamb?" He, too, has complete faith in God and also in his father. He goes along with his father's instructions and accepts his father's words. He is already a grown person; according to some calculations, he is thirty-seven years old at the time of the Akedah; according to others, he is twenty-seven. I believe that we should not accept literally the ages of Abraham, Sarah, and Isaac as recorded in the Bible. The main thing is that the biblical account stresses that all these people are mature. By the time this episode takes place, they have had many of life's experiences along with the opportunity to integrate these experiences into wisdom. As for Isaac, it seems obvious that he is meant to be understood as young by comparison to his father, but old enough to grant his consent to what his father is about to do.

Isaac appears here and in subsequent chapters of Genesis as not a passive person; but, on the other hand, he is not as active as either his father or his son Jacob. He will eventually be distinguished for his serenity, kindness, domestic joy, and his searches for water in the thirsty lands of the Middle East.*

Certain key problems remain to be discussed. Why does God subject Abraham to such a test? What does He want to prove? What can a test of such magnitude signify? What does Isaac represent in this story? He represents many things, but in my opinion the main one is *love*. When God announces to Abraham the forthcoming test, He refers to Isaac as "Thine only son, whom thou lovest." Indeed Abraham loves other people, too, but Isaac, his only son after the dismissal of Ishmael, occupies the preponderant role in Abraham's heart, and Isaac is irreplaceable because it is from him that a nation is to be generated.

The love that Abraham has for Isaac is one that subsumes the various types of love a human being can experience: family love, for Isaac is his son; love for one's neighbor (or for the other), for Isaac is a fellow human being; self-love, for Isaac is his only son and one of the most meaningful parts of Abraham's life; love for work and ideals, for Abraham has concentrated in Isaac most of his care and concern; love for life, not only because Isaac is a living human being but the one from whom the great family of Abraham will descend and be perpetuated. Isaac is expected to be the progenitor of a great people, chosen to give to the world Abraham's revelation of the One God, the God of Love who cannot be seen but is everywhere.

Thus, love for Isaac does not mean only love for Isaac, but for everything that is meaningful to Abraham—and especially love for humanity, which through Isaac and Isaac's descendants will be blessed by the knowledge of God. God has said to Abraham, "And I will make of thee a great nation, and I will bless thee, and make thy name great, . . .

* Genesis 26:32–33.

and in thee shall all the families of the earth be blessed." *
All the families of the earth will be blessed. The love for
God that Abraham has revealed after discovering Him or
having the intuition of Him, will from now on pass to mankind through the knowledge and ways that Abraham will
transmit to the generations after. Abraham's love will thus
be transmitted as a blessing to all the families of the earth.
What greater possible love? In the context of the whole
episode Abraham's love for Isaac comes to be the equivalent, or almost, of love for anything and everything God
makes us love. But to love anything and everything that
God makes us love is to love God.

By making such an enormous request of Abraham, who
is the first on earth to discover love for the One and Imageless God, God compells him to see the limitless dimensions
of such love. Once Abraham understands the magnitude of
this love for God, God stops him. "Abraham, Abraham . . .
Lay not thine hand upon the lad, neither do thou any thing
unto him." Thus what starts as a supposed sacrifice of Isaac
ends by being only an "akedah," a "binding of Isaac." The
"binding of Isaac," the name by which the story has been
known in the Hebrew tradition, may mean not only that
Isaac is bound as part of the supposed sacrificial procedure,
but also that he is bound to the greatest possible love, love
of God.

But why would God want to show in this way how
great and demanding is the love of God? Because Abraham
is the first one on earth who experiences it, he is the first
Jew, and he has to transmit to his descendants how important and all-inclusive is such a love. The whole spirituality
of humanity has its foundation in this love. And this love
requires full commitment, and any sacrifice. Without such

* Genesis 12:2–3.

love the whole world would remain a world of idolaters and pagans.

As we have seen in chapter 1, with the intuition of the one imageless God, Abraham has separated the physical world from the spiritual. It is especially love, and in particular love of God, which could reunite again the two worlds in perfect fusion and arrest entropy (chapter 2). Isaac, in being a human being, has a physical body and thus can represent the physical world; but he is also a highly spiritual human being, and in the act of the would-be sacrifice has to be bound to God's love.

In my opinion, the Jewish tradition according to which this trial of Abraham represents the commitment, the willingness, the readiness to sacrifice everything for the love of God that the Jewish people had to possess through the ages, from Abraham to our present day, is a correct interpretation; in the more than three thousand years that have passed since the Akedah, many millions of Jews have given their lives—as Isaac is ready to do—to keep their faith and the love of God. Many Jews could not sustain the heavy burden, chose easier ways, and separated themselves from the faith of Abraham. But a few million remained, and they still hold to their faith and to their love of God. Of all the ages that have passed since the time of Abraham, in none more than ours has the Jew been made to feel the difficulty of retaining that faith, retaining that love. Nothing could have been harder both to witness and to endure than the Holocaust which took place in our century. No other era has been so impervious to such horror and anguish, no other century has been so lacking in compassion and willingness to help. And if this apparent indifference to a pain of such magnitude was not really indifference but the fear of retaliation at the hands of the tyrant, no other fear has so eclipsed compassion, love, and the love of God. No other century has shown more how much the love of God, and with it goodness and abhorrence of evil, are needed on earth.

In biblical times the prophets interpret the historical disasters that befell the Jews as punishment for their having strayed from the law of God. Their interpretation may once have been correct. It is my personal opinion, however—which I know might be wrong—that the present generation of people descended from Abraham by blood and spirit, and also those descended from him in spirit only, should feel that what happened to the Jews in this century was not a punishment for lack of faith, but something extremely grave which happened to them precisely because they, or their parents, or their grandparents *kept* the faith of Abraham, and sustained Abraham's love of God. Thus, if the disaster of our century has to be compared to a biblical event, it should be compared not to the other tragic events described by the prophets, but to the would-be sacrifice of Isaac. The greatest of all of God's requests—that Abraham sacrifice Isaac—ends with a demonstration of how enormous and all-embracing our love for God should be. The greatest of all of Hitler's evil ended with the extermination of one-third of the Jewish people and demonstrated how truly enormous evil can be. The greatness of love for God, however, proved to be greater even than this greatest of evils. It is true that six million Jews, out of eighteen million, perished. It is as if one-third of Isaac had been sacrificed. The comparison of course, is faulty because one-third of a person cannot be sacrificed. Isaac does not perish; and the faith of Abraham does not perish. In a world like our present one, in which values tend to be eclipsed or minimized, where evil prevails, either in the form of persecution and discrimination or of crime and terrorism, there is great need of faith and love of God. The descendants of Abraham by blood who have survived, and the descendants of Abraham in spirit only, who have not been totally brutalized or made impervious by the horrors of our time, must keep the faith of Abraham, and the love of God, in a time of such need.

By faith and the love of God, I do not mean necessarily the practice of the rituals of a cult, which may not be possible for some people to do. Faith and the love of God may mean only to maintain that spirituality to which we refer in chapter 2. And yet in spite of the contemporary tragedy, this faith and love of God does not seem to have increased.

Nevertheless, Isaac is saved. We have to save him again and again and again, through our repeated allegiance, through our commitment, through our faith, through our love of God. Science, unless it is reconnected with values, is not the solution to the predicament of the modern world. Science has enlarged the realm of the visible—with the electromicroscope—and it has divided the atom that only a short time ago was deemed indivisible. But let us remember that we must accept the invisible, visible only in its effects, and let us make a unity of what can be divided —not a fictitious unity that pleases only those who cannot divide and reunite, but a union formed by what must be *bound* together, like spirit and matter, like the body of Isaac and infinite love.

GOD'S CHANCE

A few issues remain to be discussed in connection with the Akedah. We must consider again certain aspects of the role of God in this story. If I speak about God in human terms, it is only because I am compelled to use my human experience. I have no desire to anthropomorphize God; however, I have to use the words that are at my disposal, and these words generally are fit only for human needs in a secular world. Does God know the outcome of the Akedah in advance? If He knows that Abraham will pass the test, why does He have to subject Abraham to it? On the other hand, if it is predetermined that Abraham will please God, why would we attribute merit to Abraham?

I do not profess to have more than my own opinion on these questions. I have never found it easy to understand how it is possible for one to reconcile the concept of free will with the idea that God knows the outcome in advance. Moreover, other passages of the Bible suggest that God does *not* know how a man will choose to act. Notions of divine grace and predestination—stressed by Augustine and Martin Luther—are not natural to Judaism. At the beginning of the twelfth century the Roman Catholic Anselm tried to find a solution to this problem by stating that God's predestination takes into account human will and does not control it. He grants grace to those of whose good will He knows beforehand. This is a play on words. How can He know that a will is good if the will is free?

The Book of Jonah indicates that man enjoys free will, not grace of predestination. From a moral point of view, the human being is not at the mercy of blind fatalism. God tells Jonah to announce to the city of Nineveh that the city will be destroyed because its inhabitants have sinned in a terrible way. After trying to escape from this mission, Jonah reluctantly delivers the message. The inhabitants of Nineveh, hearing the prophet's message, repent, and the city is saved. This unexpected outcome makes Jonah angry, as we have discussed in chapter 3. Jonah had gone to Nineveh as the bearer of an inviolable decree, but in an act of love God accepts the community of Nineveh back into His heart. At the same time Jonah thinks that God has made a liar out of him and out of Himself. Does the biblical text indicate that God lies? Obviously not. There is another possible interpretation. Even God does not know that the people of Nineveh, from the most to the least important of them, will repent. The people of Nineveh have been terrible sinners, and the probability is great that they will not listen to Jonah's message and will continue to sin. But they do listen. The extremely improbable, unknown even to God, occurs, and they repent. God thus changes His plan and the city is saved.

Absolute predictability is possible only in a deterministic world. But with the creation of man in the image of God, human will emerged. With the creation of man, God relinquished part of His omniscience.

In the case of Abraham, too, God takes a chance. Since Abraham has free will, God cannot be absolutely sure that he will pass the test. However, in this case God takes a favorable chance. I hope I do not offend if I say, anthropomorphically, that God has a good bet. To borrow the terms used by Socrates * in a completely different context, for Abraham to do otherwise would be to be out of harmony with himself and to contradict himself. What we know about the previous events of Abraham's life do not give us certainty but suggest to us that most probably Abraham will act in accordance with God's request. It is true that he argues with God in the defense of Sodom and Gomorrah, but in that circumstance he is a defender of others, not of his own personal love or interests.

At God's request he has left his father's home and his

* Plato, *Gorgias* 482 c.

country. He allows his nephew Lot to take the best part of the land, when the land has to be divided to provide sustenance to both of them. The whole previous life of Abraham has been devoted to love of God and to love of his fellow human beings.

So Abraham remains in harmony with himself, and the chance that God takes proves good. Abraham passes the test and his progeny become the people of Israel. The Midrash says that God tests only the strong. Abraham is blessed in the most far-reaching way possible. With the Angel acting as intermediary God says

> "By myself I have sworn because you have done this, and have not withheld your son, your only son, I will indeed bless you, and I will multiply your descendants as the stars of heaven and as the sand which is on the seashore . . . and by your descendants shall all the nations of the earth bless themselves, because you have obeyed my voice."

Abraham is blessed in the greatest possible way. After all, again being anthropomorphic, we can say that God needs Abraham. Abraham makes God known on earth. Before Abraham, we can imagine God alone in whatever we conceive of as Heaven or the transcendental world—alone, without a place yet in the human heart. Abraham is the first partner and friend. Thus, God takes a favorable chance with Abraham. God, too, has faith in Abraham; it is not just that Abraham has faith in God.

Did God have faith in man when He created him? Was the risk that God took well taken when He created free will as part of the advent of man, in a predominantly deterministic world? If we have faith in God, we must believe that ultimately, God's risk is well taken. However, the events of our century—two major world wars, the massacre of two million Armenians, a conspicuous number of lesser wars, the use of the atomic bomb, and most of all the Holocaust destroying six million innocent civilians, of whom one million were children—incline us to believe that that question is still debatable. Man must deserve his freedom. History is the result of this freedom. If the whole world, including human beings, were ineluctably to follow a deterministic iron law, there would be no evil. There would be no good either. We would be in a world without values.

Apparently in order to have a world with values we must risk evil. The Holocaust bespeaks the full potentiality of evil within the framework of human free will. As I wrote in *The Parnas,*

Society at large has not yet acquired sufficient knowledge of the Holocaust, and twentieth-century culture has not yet absorbed its whole meaning. The destiny of mankind may to a large extent depend on the understanding that future generations have of the Holocaust and on the way they respond to this new awareness of the full potentiality of evil. If oblivion or undue permissiveness are allowed to hide the knowledge that what was called the Final Solution was to a considerable extent accomplished, man may move toward another and greater and realistically possible Final Solution for which there will be no chosen people, but for which all people will be chosen. Will this be man's last choice? *We must believe that it will not be.* For if awareness of the full potentiality of evil is acquired, mankind will not allow a similar event ever again to darken the earth. The greater the evil, the greater must be the understanding and the love to undo that evil.*

* Silvano Arieti, *The Parnas* (New York: Basic Books, 1979), pp. 152–53.

The Jewish people has been chosen again; in this twentieth century, they have been *chosen* to face the greatest possible evil, the greatest ever to appear on earth. The Jewish people, the victims of this evil, must now choose to remind the world of its potentiality; they must remind the world over and over again in every possible way. The destiny of mankind depends on our ability to understand, to control, or to prevent evil.

The Jewish people must also invite all the other peoples of the earth to nourish the greater love that is required to undo the existing evil. "Love thy God with all thy heart and all thy soul." * "Love thy neighbor as thyself." † For whatever arduous test it will require, for whatever offer of love it will demand, the example of the patriarch Abraham, father of all of us, will be with us. Thus God will not be alone. The Jewish people, and whoever may join them in the arduous task, may recognize themselves as once again chosen to diminish God's great risk, to be again, like Abraham, God's great friends and allies.

It is by the choosing that we become again and again a chosen people. Lest these words appear arrogant, or even offensive, to non-Jews, I wish to explain what I mean by the term "chosen people." I do believe that every people has been chosen to play a special role in the history of mankind; but the people themselves must choose to be chosen to play that particular role. And let me stress this: few are the people who have not considered themselves chosen, or who have not chosen to be chosen to play a particular role. The Jews may have found this role for them openly announced in the Bible, and may now consider to choose

* Deuteronomy 6:5.
† Leviticus 19:17.

to be chosen to reveal to the world the full potentiality of evil and the love required to undo the evil.

Most people of the earth, or most groups of people, and not only the Jews, have considered themselves chosen to play a historical and/or transcendental role. The ancient Greeks considered themselves the only people on earth chosen to represent man in his full rational capacity; all others were barbarians. The Romans came to include themselves along with the Greeks among those chosen not to be barbarians. Moreover, they saw themselves, as Virgil and other writers describe, as destined to rule the world with Roman law. The Christians have regarded themselves among all believers as chosen for salvation. Departing from the Jewish faith, and by contrast with the teachings of other religions, they believe that only with baptism in the name of Christ can a man be chosen for access to the door of Heaven. All the others are barren, cannot be chosen. Frenchmen, even before the Revolution but especially after it, gave central importance to the role French culture was chosen to play in Western civilization. Voltaire (1694–1778) called France *"la deuxième patrie de tout hommes civilizés"* ("the second fatherland of every civilized man").

John Foxe (1516–87) saw in English history the great work of Christian salvation. Hegel (1770–1831) saw in German history the fulfillment of the greatness of the human spirit. Vincenzo Gioberti (1802–1852) saw the primacy of Italy among all the nations of the world, and Giuseppe Mazzini (1805–1872) saw in Italian history proof of the religious mission of the Italian people. Until recently practically all Americans believed that the United States was destined to enable human beings to achieve a new and higher level of human fulfillment. America's Puritan heritage conferred the feeling that both as individuals and as a nation Americans have a special mission. In his book *Redeemer Nation: The Idea of America's Millennial Role,* Tuveson * stresses the concept of America's holy destiny. In *The Puritan Origins of the American Self,* Bercovitch † holds that the great migration from England to New England had the same significance for the colonials as the return to the land of Israel had for the Jews who had been in Babylonian captivity. In an excellent article, from which I have borrowed some ideas about the American heritage, the educator M. M. Marsden ‡ writes that Ralph Waldo Emerson thought God took the mission of America so seriously that He had kept the American continent "on reserve from intellectual races until they should grow up to it." "When the proper time had arrived," Marsden summarizes Emerson, "Boston had been appointed by God in the destiny of nations to lead civilization." Marsden reminds us that President Wilson described America's mission in the First World War and its aftermath as the "redemption of the world." He further reminds us that in his testimony to the Senate Foreign Relations Committee on 20 February 1967, the eminent historian Henry Steele Commager stressed a

> deep and persistent trait of the American mind: the belief in Old World corruption and New World innocence. The men who won the independence of America from the mother country were convinced that the Old World was abandoned to tyranny, misery, ignorance, injustice and vice, and that the New World was innocent of these sins.

* Ernest Lee Tuveson, *Redeemer Nation: The Idea of America's Millennial Role* (Chicago: University of Chicago Press, 1968).

† Sacvan Bercovitch, *The Puritan Origins of the American Self* (New Haven: Yale University Press, 1975).

‡ M. M. Marsden, "Disenchantment and Apple Pie: Our Unique American Heritage," *The Elmira Review* (1979) pp. 4-12.

It is this American Dream which, together with Puritan attitudes, has induced Americans to consider themselves superior to others, to see in their history a Manifest Destiny, and see themselves chosen to assert the American Way. Thus Americans, too, as a people have seen themselves as chosen. True, Marsden also notes that in recent years this point of view has been challenged. Many eminent thinkers no longer believe in the American Way.

Marsden, if I understand him correctly, does not seem willing to accept this new anti-missionary sense of America. I hope nobody does. If America should give up the vision of herself as chosen to fulfill a chosen mission, it would be only because we have allowed those destructive forces reported in chapter 2 to prevail. Each group, each nation, each faith, retains its feeling of special chosenness as long as its ideals do not decay or are not substituted for by inferior ones, and as long as the actions of its members are commensurate to what were their highest values and highest possibilities for love.

CHAPTER

V

Abraham, Avinu

Sacrifice of Iphigenia (fresco in Pompey)

Hearken to me, you who pursue deliverance, you who seek the Lord; look to the rock from which you were hewn, and to the quarry from which you were digged. Look to Abraham your father and to Sarah who bore you; for when he was but one I called him and I blessed him and made him many.*

With these words, received from God, Isaiah reminds the Jewish people of their origin. The knowledge of the solidarity of their origin should revamp their faith.

The past is not dead; it may temporarily be dead in our hearts and memories, ready to be rekindled and to inspire us again. Throughout Jewish history Abraham is called *Avinu*, our father; Moses is *Rabenu*, our teacher. The paternal role of Abraham is stressed throughout Jewish history and is stressed also in the Christian religion. Saint Paul writes, "I myself am an Israelite, a descendant of Abraham, a member of the tribe of Benjamin."

The fatherhood of Abraham raises several issues. First is his relation with his own father, Terah. God tells Abraham, "Get thee out of thy country, and from thy kindred, and from thy father's house."

Those who accept Kierkegaard's concept of the "teleological suspension of the ethical" see these words as another example of the concept. In fact, in order to follow God,

* Isaiah 51:1-2.

Abraham ceases to honor his father. Thus he goes against what will later be one of the Ten Commandments, and therefore acts unethically. What is involved is the so-called suspension of the ethical, discussed in chapter 4. Is it really unethical for Abraham to leave his father's house? Terah, although Abraham's biological father, belongs to another world, the world of idolatry. Being a mortal, Abraham needs a male parent; but spiritually he is a self-made man, he develops a new vision of the world, a new way of thinking on account of which life and the world come to be interpreted in different ways. As Isaiah wrote, he is the rock and quarry from which the Hebrews were hewn and digged. He is the one from whom the many came. He is *Avinu*, our father. We have seen in chapter 2 that he has a serious conflict with his father about what is for him, Abraham, the most fundamental issue. Were we to interpret the matter from a purely psychoanalytic point of view, we could say that Abraham rejects his own earthly father and substitutes for him the Heavenly Father. We may think that did he not undergo the conflict with his father, his whole subsequent history would be different. For those who adhere to this point of view I have to repeat what I said about Polish's interpretation of the Akedah (pp. 143–46). Even if Abraham does need this family conflict in order to actualize his mission later, that mission must not be interpreted solely or mainly in the light of that original conflict. The outcome is what matters, not the beginning or the original psychological motive—the outcome that makes Abraham one of the most important figures in the history of humanity.

He who rejects his father, and who according to the Midrash is rejected by his own father, becomes the father of all Jews. And yet in order to prove that he can become the father of all Jews, he has to prove his willingness to give up the son he most loves. By following God's instruction, he prepares the blueprint for the history of the whole Jewish people. "Get thee out of thy country, and from thy kindred, and from thy father's house." How many times has this happened to the children of Israel! How many of us relive in these words what took place in our own lives. I, too, recognize myself in these words, getting out of the country of my birth, Italy, and from my kindred—the people among whom for several centuries my ancestors had lived—and, in spite of my love for him and my mother, from my father's house, when Mussolini extended to Italy the Nazi miasma. Abraham feels he was in exile, as Jews have felt so often throughout their history when they were among people who did not want to accept them—and even persecuted them—because of their different beliefs.

In chapter 17 of Genesis the famous covenant between God and Abraham is described. Abraham is now ninety-nine. God appears to him and says:

> "I am God Almighty; walk before me, and be you whole. And I will make my covenant between me and you, and you will multiply exceedingly." Then Abraham fell on his face; and God said to him, "Behold, my covenant is with you, and you shall be the father of a multitude of nations. I will make you exceedingly fruitful; and I will make nations of you, and kings shall come forth from you. And I will establish my covenant between me and you and your descendants after you throughout their generations for an everlasting covenant, to be God to you and to your descendants after you. And I will give to you, and to your descendants after you, the land of your sojournings, all the

land of Canaan, for an everlasting possession; and I will be their God."

And God said to Abraham:

"As for you, you shall keep my covenant, you and your descendants after you throughout their generations. This is my covenant, which you shall keep, between me and you and your descendants after you: Every male among you shall be circumcised.

"You shall be circumcised in the flesh of your foreskins, and it shall be a sign of the covenant between me and you. He that is eight days old among you shall be circumcised. . . . So shall my covenant be in your flesh an everlasting covenant. Any uncircumcised male who is not circumcised in the flesh of his foreskin shall be cut off from his people; he has broken my covenant."

Why is circumcision so important? The ancient Hebrews could not know the medical reasoning that recommends it. Circumcision has to be considered literally and meta-phorically. The metaphorical aspect, strangely, is easier to explain: throughout the Old Testament being uncircumcised means to have a heart not open to feelings or to good influence, or not to be responsive to the voice of God.

In a second covenant that God made with Moses, God says, " 'the Lord your God will circumcise your heart and the heart of your offspring, so that you will love the Lord your God with all your heart, and with all your soul.' " *
In Exodus, when God commands Moses to go to speak to Pharaoh and he is reluctant to go, he says apologetically, " 'I am of uncircumcised lips,' " † meaning that he was not a good speaker—in fact, he was a stutterer. The prophet

---

* Deuteronomy 30:6.
† Exodus 6:30.

Jeremiah says, "Their ears are uncircumcised; they cannot listen; behold, the word of the Lord is to them an object of scorn, they take no pleasure in it." * Later Jeremiah calls the house of Israel "uncircumcised in heart" † because it does not follow the way of God.

Circumcision, although easy to perform, may appear indeed a heavy imposition to people who are not used to it. Saint Paul saw in it a great obstacle to proselytism if Christianity were to adopt it, and attacked it on various grounds: to observe the law of God is as good as to be circumcised, even if we are not ("if a man who is uncircumcised keeps the precepts of the law, will not his uncircumcision be regarded as circumcision?" ‡). Later he wrote, "For he is not a real Jew who is one outwardly, nor is true circumcision something external and physical. He is a Jew who is one inwardly, and real circumcision is a matter of the heart, spiritual and literal." § Paul thus seems to agree with all the writers of the Old Testament that circumcision of the foreskin is not enough; but whereas they believe that physical circumcision is also necessary, he is ready to dismiss it in spite of Abraham's covenant.

Why is circumcision necessary also in its physical actuality? I believe that, again, this is to be interpreted in the context of that particular type of dualism which is characteristic of the Jewish tradition. The body is different from the spirit but must interact with, and in turn be interacted with by the spirit. At the moment that Abraham recognizes God and thus divides spirit from matter, his interest becomes one of joining matter to the spirit of God. Although the spiritual is the main concern, the corporeal

* Jeremiah 6:10.
† Jeremiah 9:10.
‡ Romans 2:25.
§ Romans 2:28–29.

is not to be despised. Life in the flesh, too, has to be sanctified. Marriage is blessed; sexual life with one's spouse is beautiful. Circumcision is a way of spiritualizing the body, or reuniting the two parts of man. Women cannot be circumcised, but the circumcision of the male members of the family is enough to maintain Abraham's covenant in the whole family.

Saint Paul's disrespect for circumcision is consistent with what he thought about the body and the flesh. Especially in the letter to the Romans, he shows his great contempt for whatever belongs to the flesh. He thus begins a type of dualism which will continue and become even more pronounced in Augustine and other great medieval writers of the Roman Catholic Church.

Throughout Western civilization this demarcation between body and spirit, matter and soul, brain and psyche, will be accentuated to such an extreme as to eventuate in our present-day revolt against any dualism. But it is only this extremism that stimulates the revolt. A counterbalance, an equilibrium, must be maintained, and interaction must be implemented. The body must be sanctified, and the spirit must also pay attention to the mundane affairs of the world.

Since the acceptance of harmonized dualism or interactionism is one of the major theses of this book, I must take up again what I have discussed in previous chapters and add a few more considerations. An extreme dualism or forced separation between matter and spirit may not only end in monistic positions that see man as only spirit or as only flesh, but may lead us also to fantastic philosophies and ideologies or to satiric expressions of art. I shall give a few and quick examples.

For Bishop Berkeley (1685–1753), the great "immaterialist," nothing but minds and their ideas exist. To be is to be perceived (ideas) or to be a perceiver (mind). Whatever exists or is real, is a conscious mind or perceptions and ideas held by minds. No physical reality exists. The flesh which was sin, or potentially inducive of sin for Saint Paul, becomes nonexistent for Berkeley. Hegel (1770–1831) is at times called the founder of an absolute or monistic idealism. Actually he speaks about the environment and its interrelation with the self in a dynamic process. Nature is the Absolute Reason which manifests itself in external form. Extremist idealism denies the physical world, becomes excessively optimistic, and does not confront adequately the problem of evil.

In reaction to this idealistic extremism, the materialistic conception of the universe emerges. For mechanistic materialism, everything can be explained with the laws that rule matter and motion. The world is an unlimited material entity, in which everything is purposeless and meaningless. Two great exponents of materialism, Marx (1818–1883) and Engels (1820–1875), accept Hegel's methodology by reversing his position. According to them, matter, mainly through the economic organization of society and the modes of production, shapes the social and political institutions of mankind. Values tend to be seen only as expression of the forces of production. Religion becomes "the opiate of the people."

The so-called English physiocrats (Adam Smith, Thomas Malthus, and David Ricardo), who lived between the end of the eighteenth century and the beginning of the nineteenth, also see political, social, and economic phenomena as governed by natural laws. But these natural laws, and the laissez faire attitude, have eventually led to the accumulation of power in the hands of few, to the corporative society, and to empty consumerism.

These are only a few examples. Whether the basic issues are religious, political, social, or historical, many errors or excesses are attributable to the fact that the balance has tipped either toward a predominantly materialistic dualism, which may become monistic materialism, or toward an excessively idealistic dualism, which may become a monistic idealism. Many religions, too, have tilted in one direction or the other. They have proclaimed that history is not their field, and that they intend to remain in the realm of the spiritual; but their clericalism has become much concerned with history. The condition of a religion has often been determined by military power, as in the case of Constantine,* by its relation with the power elite, or by stress on external formalism.

The way in which the individual idealist can become grotesque, ridiculous, bizarre, or "quixotic" is typified in Don Quixote himself, the fabulous character created by Cervantes. In his idealism Don Quixote refuses to see reality, insists that windmills are giants and that barbers' washbasins are the helmets of heroes. We are more inclined to agree with Don Quixote's servant Sancho Panza, who rides on a donkey and hence on reality. But the reality seen from the saddle of the donkey of Sancho Panza, it is to be hoped, is not a reality that fully reflects the world or our own aspirations. Perhaps man's common practice, when he aims at highest values, is to do so in a quixotic way, to be corrected by a Sancho Panza, or vice versa.

---

* With Constantine the following rule was adopted: "*Eius religio cuius regio.*" ("The religion of the country must be that of the person to whom the country belongs, either emperor or king").

But even a worse state than being in the Quixote-Sancho Panza dilemma is to have no dilemma at all—to have accepted a purely monistic life where the only thing that counts is to consume and to experience immediate and transient pleasure. All the rest is fiction, all the rest is trimming. Another, and even worse, solution is to believe that the world is purposeless and meaningless. According to this view, man cannot reconcile himself with the inhuman state of his human existence; he is still waiting for Godot and tries to deny the absurd universe in absurd ways. For him the rose that opens the beauty and fragrance of its petals into the air of May is meaningless, the waves of the sea that break over the rocks are meaningless, the wind and the rain are meaningless, the network of billions of neurons that constitutes our brain is meaningless. Beethoven's notes are meaningless, and Shakespeare's sonnets could be written by a monkey on a typewriter over millions of years by randomly pressing the letters—and a monkey who would do so for trillions of years could perhaps type even the *Divine Comedy, Paradise Lost,* and the *Iliad* and the *Odyssey*. Any love is meaningless; or perhaps there is no love, and with the word love we mask our ugly nature. The love of the swallow who brings food to her fledgling, the love of the mother who caresses and embraces her baby, are also masks for ugly needs.

A person who sees the world in this way cannot silence the earthly sounds and hear the Eternal voice. He cannot even see the harmony in the physical universe but sees only furious and random collisions of atoms which a God-less time has tamed in some sporadic spots throughout the passage of eons. He is alone, anguished, and bewildered, an orphan forever, aimless and lost in the abysmal and heartless cosmos. But no orphan will be he who, even in this

tragic twentieth century, follows the father of some ancient and most modern men, Abraham from the land of Ur,
the dualist and interactionist who by indicating to us how
to attune the earthly to the Imageless Transcendence, led
us to hear "Love thy God with all thy heart and all thy
soul" and "Love thy neighbor as thyself."

INDEX

Index

Index

Index